UNIQUE EATS AND EATERIES

OF

SAN FRANCISCO

Kimberley Lovato

Library of Congress Control Number: 2017934683
ISBN: 9781681061115

Printed in the United States of America
17 18 19 20 21   5 4 3 2 1

DEDICATION

To San Francisco and all who love her.

CONTENTS

ACKNOWLEDGMENTS

Thanks go out to all my friends who put up with me (and barely saw me) while I wrote this book—dinner's on me! To my daughter, Chloe, and my husband, John, who never stop encouraging me to do what I love. To my mother and editorial assistant, Salle, who kept me organized while praising every word I wrote, as if each were laced in truffle butter. And to the restaurateurs, chefs, owners, and food makers who let me pick your brain—thank you. You put the sweet foggy icing on our already delightful San Francisco cake.

INTRODUCTION

In another career that involved cubicles and quarterly reports, a colleague sat on my linoleum desk and asked me the question that would ultimately lead to the writing of this book: "What would you do, professionally, if you could do anything?" The answer came immediately. "I'd write." Working beside me for years, he'd witnessed me frowning and rubbing my temples, and my career frustration hadn't escaped him. He stood up and put a hand on my shoulder. "Do it," he said. "Go find what you love and fill up on it." Twenty years later, not a day goes by that I don't feel grateful for that conversation. Today, I write for a living, and it never gets old—especially when it combines three things I love to muse over—people, places, and food. When the opportunity to pen *Unique Eats and Eateries of San Francisco* came along, I couldn't say no. San Francisco is, for me, a place where food and people are inextricably linked. It's Zuni Café, where my husband, my best friend, and I laughed for hours one afternoon. It's the taqueria my daughter and I call on the way home from the airport after traveling. It's fresh Dungeness crab on New Year's Eve and fresh pasta and sauce from Lucca Ravioli so I can impress my Italian in-laws. It's The Grove, where I had my first "date" with one of my now-closest friends. It's hundreds more meals and memories. Ask any San Franciscan and he or she has a numinous devotion to a different worthy list. Indeed, San Francisco is full of enthusiastic eaters willing to wait an hour or more in line for their favorite food. How can one not be intrigued by a city that buzzes at this level of culinary velocity? This book is not a "best of" book. This is a book about what fuels the zeal: the gutsy chefs and benevolent restaurateurs, the revelatory food, the classic dishes, and the iconic restaurants whose diverse backstories make our city a textured, three-dimensional, world-class dining destination. While I was writing this book, a common theme emerged: the pursuit of "soulful endeavors," as Tawla's owner, Azhar Hashem, so elegantly stated. Azhar left a stellar career at Google to bring the food of her Jordanian childhood to her adopted city. Todd Masonis sold his tech company and paved his future path in chocolate. Roland Passot launched his now-Michelin-starred French restaurant with a little savings and a name—La Folie—sparked by his wife's comment that he must be crazy to start a restaurant in San Francisco. Then there were the people behind Bi-Rite Market, Mission Pie, and Saint Frank Coffee, who live and work by the ethos of supporting communities, farmers, and families. Literally thousands more like them populate this city, all committed to their own soulful endeavors. I wish I could tell you about each of them, because each must have a worthy tale. But I hope *Unique Eats and Eateries of San Francisco* serves up a toothsome slice of this uncommonly edible city and whets your appetite to come and find what you love, and fill up on it. —KL

UNIQUE EATS AND EATERIES

OF

SAN FRANCISCO

1300 ON FILLMORE

The soul of the Fillmore

L isten closely and you can almost hear the saxophone riffs and
half-time tempo of musical legends who once roamed the streets
of the city's Historic Fillmore Jazz Preservation District (a.k.a. the
Fillmore). At its revitalized heart is 1300 on Fillmore. Helmed by
chef David Lawrence and his wife, Monetta White, whose mother
and grandmother grew up nearby, the restaurant sits in what was
once the sizzling epicenter of jazz during the 1940s and 1950s.

Not only is 1300 on Fillmore one of the few African American-
owned businesses in the neighborhood, but it also proudly pays
homage to San Francisco's jazz age, something Monetta says was
essential to the design of the restaurant.

Take a stroll down memory lane in the restaurant's Heritage
Lounge, with its eye-catching collage of framed and backlit black-
and-white photos of performers who frequented the district in
its heyday.

The dreamy space hosts live entertainment, but it's David's classic
culinary training, Jamaican roots, and refined Southern taste that are
the real draw. Dive into a menu of irresistible bites, such as cornbread
with pepper jelly, crispy fried chicken, and barbecue shrimp and

---

The nearby Fillmore Auditorium has hosted James Brown,
Ike and Tina Turner, and thousands of other musical acts.

Top right: Southern-inspired food, such as fried chicken, is on the menu. Photo courtesy of 1300 on Fillmore

Above left: Chef David Lawrence and Monetta White. Photo courtesy of 1300 on Fillmore

Above right: The Heritage Lounge is an homage to the Fillmore's heyday. Photo courtesy of 1300 of Fillmore

creamy grits so good you'll want to sing. But save that for 1300 on Fillmore's famous Sunday Gospel Brunch, where jazz history sings alongside bananas Foster, French toast, and the cinnamon-dusted beignets.

1300 Fillmore St.
415-771-7100
www.1300fillmore.com
Neighborhood: Fillmore

AL's PLACE

Veggie delights

Even if you prefer your dinner plate piled with slow-simmered meat or anything wrapped in bacon, you'll still find it hard not to swoon over AL's Place, whose innovative menu moves vegetables into the spotlight and puts meat on the side. It's not conventional, but then nothing about Aaron London trends mainstream.

From the time he got his first kitchen job at fourteen to obtaining his degree at The Culinary Institute of America, Aaron's star has been on the rise. AL's Place (AL stands for Aaron London) is the first solo endeavor from the former chef of Napa's beloved yet bygone vegetarian restaurant, Ubuntu, an address that earned a Michelin star under Aaron's toque and earned him a James Beard Award nomination for Rising Star Chef. The restaurant's closure set the stage for an eighteen-month bicycle trip through Europe, mostly in France, where Aaron pedaled through wine regions, followed his nose down gravel paths, and staged in several coveted kitchens.

His food today is influenced by all the places he's traveled, and his resume reads like a passport with stamps from restaurants in Japan, Thailand, Montreal, and New York. San Francisco has him now. He opened the forty-nine-seat AL's Place in 2015 with a menu of "snackles" that include brine-pickled French fries (yes, they are amazing) and vadouvan almonds, and a rotation of must-be-tasted-to-be-believed mains such as grits with eight-hour fava beans or asparagus with green peach mayo.

> "When people tell me, 'Nobody does that,'
> I always say, 'Well, somebody has to be first.'"
> ~Aaron London

Top left: Aaron London, chef and owner of AL's Place. Photo courtesy of Molly DeCoudreaux

Top right: The decor is airy and bright to match the fresh menu. Photo courtesy of Molly DeCoudreaux

Above left: The food is not just good for you but also good to look at. Photo courtesy of Molly DeCoudreaux

Above right: The pickled (yes, pickled) French fries are not to be missed. Photo courtesy of Molly DeCoudreaux

So much personality, creativity, and passion are there that *Bon Appétit* magazine recognized AL's Place as the country's Best New Restaurant of its inaugural year. Aaron says he remembers the moment well. As the names on the list slowly whittled down to the top ten, he says he was already honored. A request for a photo shoot had him growing hopeful enough to book out the bar, just in case. When the morning arrived, Aaron says he continuously refreshed the *Bon Appétit* website, waiting for the results. As soon as it was announced, reservations blew up, and three years later business is still steady. Says Aaron, "It felt like a validation, but I don't ever want to take it for granted."

1499 Valencia St.
415-416-6136
www.alsplacesf.com
Neighborhood: Mission

ALFRED'S STEAKHOUSE

San Francisco's oldest steakhouse

With only a twenty-dollar gold piece in his hand and a train ticket from New York, Alfred Bacchini set off for San Francisco in 1911, where he worked as a busboy and waiter, eventually scraping together enough money to start his own business.

In 1928, when he was just twenty-seven years old, his eponymous restaurant opened on Vallejo Street. Nearly ninety years later, it is still going strong as San Francisco's oldest steakhouse. Alfred ran it until the 1970s and then sold it to the Petri family, who kept the name but moved the restaurant from its Broadway location to Merchant Street in 1997.

In 2016, Alfred's was sold again, this time to the Daniel Patterson Group. Concerned regulars need not worry. Chef Daniel Patterson assures loyalists that the essence of Alfred's will endure along with the tufted red booths, the ruby-red walls, and the crystal chandeliers that Alfred installed, replicas of those found in the Vienna Opera House. However, things have been cleaned, dusted, and spit-shined to sparkle in a space that once housed the venerated Blue Fox Restaurant. Nowhere else in San Francisco can you find such grandness in a steakhouse, with its expansive lobby, coat closet, and a plush decor evoking the vintage glamour found in old movies and memories.

> Martinis and manhattans are made tableside, and the shaker is left with guests. It's probably the biggest drink pour in the city.

Left: Old-world glamour for an old-school steakhouse. Photo courtesy of Alanna Hale

Right: The menu is full of modernized steakhouse classics. Photo courtesy of Alanna Hale

The Blue Fox rollicked in San Francisco for fifty-one years and welcomed A-listers such as Frank Sinatra, Joe DiMaggio, and Marilyn Monroe. Alfred's still uses the original Blue Fox silver-plated bread dishes and a few other Blue Fox serving pieces. While the menu was modernized with sustainable ingredients and creativity, co-chefs Tyler Brennan and Bryan Baker deliver classic steakhouse fare. That means you can still get the oysters Rockefeller with creamed spinach, "Alfred's Cut" 28-ounce bone-in rib eye, homemade steak sauces, and bananas Foster flambéed tableside, among other old-school charms that position Alfred's for another ninety years.

659 Merchant St.
415-781-7058
www.alfredssf.com
Neighborhood: Financial District

Alioto's Rose

Long before it swarmed with map-wielding tourists and selfie sticks, Fisherman's Wharf was a nest of train tracks and lumberyards, as well as booming wholesale fisheries, which lured immigrants like Nunzio Alioto. He arrived in 1898 from Sicily and set up at fish stall #8, selling cracked crab and shrimp to other Italian workers. During this time he met and married a local girl named Rose. When Nunzio passed away suddenly at the age of forty-nine, the single mom had no choice but to roll up her sleeves, take over her husband's business, and raise her three children, Mario, Antoinette, and Frank.

Rose was the first woman to work on Fisherman's Wharf and would lay the foundation for the Alioto's of today. She installed a kitchen and officially opened Alioto's Restaurant in 1938. Rose was one of the first restaurateurs to create a fish stew called cioppino, now widely accepted as San Francisco's signature dish. Thanks to the completion of the Golden Gate and Bay Bridges in the 1930s, Fisherman's Wharf transformed into a tourist destination. The San Francisco waterfront was also a port of embarkation for sailors during World War II, and Rose served fresh seafood to servicemen and women, growing Alioto's stellar reputation.

In the 1950s she was able to expand the restaurant again, adding a second story, a move that gave Alioto's the distinction of being the tallest building on the wharf. After a fire, Rose rebuilt the restaurant on the same site. That strength of character is the reason Alioto's still stands at #8, says her granddaughter Annette Alioto, who is part of the third generation running the restaurant. She's especially proud of her grandmother, the determined matriarch whom Annette calls a

Top left: The Alioto family, with Rose on the left. Photo courtesy of Annette Alioto

Top right: At #8 on Fisherman's Wharf. Photo courtesy of Kimberley Lovato

Above left: Alioto's on Fisherman's Wharf. Photo courtesy of Fisherman's Wharf

Above right: Cioppino with a view. Photo courtesy of Annette Alioto

role model for her family and businesswomen everywhere. The menu is peppered with a number of original recipes that have survived more than ninety years, but the most popular, and rightfully so, is Nonna Rose's Famous Dungeness Crab Cioppino, flavored with a legacy that started with the dream of a young Sicilian man and continues thanks to the strength of a mighty Rose.

8 Fisherman's Wharf
415-673-0183
www.aliotos.com
Neighborhood: Fisherman's Wharf

ANCHOR BREWING COMPANY

A steam dream

Like many San Francisco stories, Anchor Brewing Company's opens during the California Gold Rush (the only brewery that has survived from that era) when immigrant Gottlieb Brekle bought a beer-and-billiards saloon in Russian Hill and began making beer under the name Golden City Brewery. A man named Ernst F. Baruth and his son-in-law purchased Golden City in 1896 and changed the name to Anchor. The brewery burned down in the 1906 earthquake, moved a few more times, and struggled to survive after Prohibition. But, like all good stories, a hero swoops in to save the day.

For Anchor Brewing Company, that was Frederick Louis "Fritz" Maytag III (of Maytag blue cheese and appliance fame). He bought the gasping facility in 1965, turning it into the nationally recognized brand it is today, with handcrafted beers made within the city limits in traditional copper kettles by current brewmaster Scott Ungermann. Scott credits his interest in beer to college (don't we all). As a Berkeley student he toured the facility with his Chi Phi fraternity brothers, calling it so pivotal a moment that he bought a home brew kit and ultimately went on to get a master's degree in brewing from UC Davis. Though he worked at Anheuser-Busch for nearly eighteen years, Anchor was always on his mind. "The initial inspiration I felt when I saw those copper kettles for the first time

> Anchor Brewing's "steam" beer name likely derived from pre-refrigeration days when San Francisco's foggy air cooled beer fermenting in warm open pans, causing it to let off steam.

Top right: When brewmaster Scott Ungermann was younger, he dreamed of working at Anchor Brewing Co. Photo courtesy of Kimberley Lovato

Above left: Anchor Brewing's original location in Russian Hill, circa 1905–1906. The building survived the 1906 earthquake but burned down during the fires that followed. Photo courtesy of Anchor Brewing Co.

Above right: Former Anchor Brewing Co. owner Frederick Louis "Fritz" Maytag is the great-grandson of Maytag Corporation founder Frederick Louis Maytag I and son of Maytag Dairy Farms founder Frederick Louis Maytag II. Photo courtesy of Anchor Brewing Co.

never left me," he says. When a job opened up with the beloved San Francisco label, he happily jumped beer ships.

In 2010 Fritz retired, and Keith Greggor, the president and CEO, now sits in Fritz's former corner office. Keith says he prefers not to think of himself as an owner but rather as a custodian of the legacy of a great San Francisco institution, a job he and the modern Anchor family take very seriously.

1705 Mariposa St.
415-863-8350
www.anchorbrewing.com
Neighborhood: Potrero Hill

* Japan's Sapporo bought Anchor Brewing in August 2017.

ASIASF

Diva-lightful

When Larry Hashbarger and Skip Young cofounded AsiaSF in 1998, they had no idea it would become an iconic San Francisco entertainment destination. It has since celebrated nearly twenty years of vibrancy, fun, and diversity, which has been a trademark of the club-restaurant since the day the Ladies of AsiaSF first sashayed down the red bar that doubles as a stage.

To date, more than one million guests have come to dine, drink, and meet the transgender stars of AsiaSF, who sing, dance, mingle, and serve the prix fixe dinners of Cal-Asian cuisine in a glossy nightclub setting. Each night features two shows, which are professionally staged by sought-after choreographer Ronnie Reddick, something that has changed since the beginning when numbers were amateurish and songs were lip-synced. Now shiny costumes, flashing lights, thumping music, and standing ovations create a theatrical experience that is San Francisco's answer to the Moulin Rouge.

Larry says he came up with the idea for AsiaSF after traveling in Southeast Asia, where he saw similar shows. He wanted to create an experience for a mainstream audience that was also a safe and celebratory place for performers. It was a hit then and now, especially with women, who make up about 70 percent of the clientele. They come for birthday bashes, reunions, bachelorette parties, or an

> "We are the essence of the San Francisco ethos
> to live your authentic life."
> ~Larry Hashbarger

Top left: AsiaSF is popular for birthday bashes and bachelorette blowouts. Photo courtesy of AsiaSF

Top right: Calamansi key lime pie. Photo courtesy of AsiaSF

Above left: Dinner and a show doesn't get more unique than AsiaSF. Photo courtesy of AsiaSF

Above right: The Ladies of AsiaSF have been celebrated since 1998. Photo courtesy of AsiaSF

unforgettable night out on the town. While it is, hands down, one of the city's most unique dining spots to fete a special occasion, AsiaSF is mostly about celebrating the diversity that San Franciscans embrace so proudly, say Larry and Skip. They hope people come with an open mind and leave with great memories, as well as the feeling of empowerment that comes from a better understanding of something that previously seemed unfamiliar.

201 Ninth St.
415-255-2742
www.asiasf.com
Neighborhood: SoMa

Morsels of memory

Growing up in India, Hetal Shah's memories are seasoned with her mom's cooking. She also recalls the opportunities she had to dine at upscale Indian restaurants in high-end hotels and the surprise she felt at discovering that home-cooked meals and street food could be sophisticated. When she moved to the United States for college, Hetal says she missed her favorite foods and special-occasion meals. To quell her homesickness, she tried a few of her mom's recipes, but Athens, Georgia, was a hard place to source the needed ingredients. August 1 Five didn't come to Hetal right away, but those morsels of childhood memory had planted their seeds.

After successful careers at major advertising companies in New York and San Francisco and six years at Google, Hetal says she was still in search of those authentic flavors, even in food-savvy San Francisco. "I felt there was a misconception of what Indian food was, and the city lacked a sophisticated take on Indian cuisine," she says. With skills she'd honed in marketing and design, Hetal took on August 1 Five, her passion project to create a modernized Indian dining experience in San Francisco.

The restaurant opened in 2016. Hetal is a vegetarian, while her husband eats everything, so the duo created a menu that caters to all preferences. Talented chef Manish Tyagi blends the freshest

August 1 Five gets its name from the date (August 15, 1947) commemorating India's independence from the British Empire.

Top: Dhokla, made from chickpea flour, is a popular snack food in India. Photo courtesy of Craig Lee

Above left: Chef Manish Tyagi creates sumptuous and modern Indian dishes. Photo courtesy of James Bueti

Above right: Hetal Shah. Photo courtesy of Luke Beard

California ingredients with traditional Indian flavors to create snacks such as gol gappa, a popular Indian street food stuffed with fresh chickpeas and potatoes; dhokla, steamed vegetarian gram flour bites; and palak chaat, a spinach appetizer topped with sweet yogurt. For meat and fish, Chef Tyagi presents items such as tandoori fish; lobster with coconut milk and curry leaves; and lamb shank with red chili, cloves, and caramelized onion.

The classic food and flavors are reinterpreted through the chef's whimsical presentation and modern cooking techniques. Served in a dining room swathed in peacock blues and teals, rich wood tones, and a hint of shimmer, the experience is, like the menu, full of surprises and delights that take Indian guests back to the taste of their childhoods, while inviting diners to discover just how sophisticated Hetal's favorite food can be.

524 Van Ness Ave.
415-771-5900
www.august1five.com
Neighborhood: Civic Center

The modern Indian dining room of August 1 Five. Photo courtesy of Patricia Chang

b. PATISSERIE

The kouign of pastries

You can practically hear the accordion notes of "La Vie en Rose" when opening the doors at this Parisian-inspired bakery that shows off the pastry panache of its owner, Belinda Leong. While her kouign amann is king, Belinda bakes a cornucopia of buttery, sweet, and savory selections every day in the open kitchen. The native San Franciscan and graduate of City College of San Francisco's hospitality program says she always enjoyed baking, but pastry was not her plan.

While working as the chef garde manger at Gary Danko, she hopped over to the pastry station when they needed help. She says she found it to be more fun and whimsical and has loved it ever since. Belinda spent eight years stunning diners at Gary Danko as the head pastry chef before venturing to Europe to stage in esteemed restaurants and patisseries, including NOMA in Copenhagen and Paris's Pierre Hermé, whose style she defines as classic modern and likens to her own. She nabbed a job at Manresa, a two-star Michelin restaurant in Los Gatos, upon her return and says she felt almost ready to open her own bakery but needed to get her name out there. Her perfected kouign amann would be her calling card. Belinda approached the best coffee shops in the city, but not many agreed to carry her baked goods. Four Barrel Coffee, Farm:Table, and a couple of small coffee shops, however, said yes, and the name Belinda Leong

> Kouign amann derives its name from the Breton words kouign (cake) and amann (butter).

Top left: Belinda Leong founded b. Patisserie in 2013. Photo courtesy of b. Patisserie

Top right: b. Patisserie. Photo courtesy of Albert Law

Above left: b. Patisserie's kouign amann. Photo courtesy of b. Patisserie

Above right: French sweet and savory pastries are a specialty. Photo courtesy of b. Patisserie

soon became synonymous with kouign amann, bostock, kugeloph, and other obscure pastries.

Belinda approached Michel Suas, founder of the San Francisco Baking Institute where she'd taken a class years earlier, in search of a partner. When he suggested himself and shared a similar vision, Belinda knew the time had come to create a French patisserie with a San Francisco soul. "I really loved how the pastries and desserts looked in the showcases in Paris, but I always thought the high-end bakeries felt too quiet and formal." B. Patisserie opened in 2013 with a friendly San Francisco swagger and a taste of France.

2821 California St.
415-440-1700
www.bpatisserie.com
Neighborhood: Pacific Heights

BEACH CHALET RESTAURANT & BREWERY

Where the park meets the Pacific

This 1925 Spanish Revival building on the western edge of Golden Gate Park has had many lives. It was originally a changing facility for Ocean Beach sunbathers and swimmers, with an upstairs bar and city-run restaurant.

During World War II, it was commandeered by the US Army, and starting in 1947 the Veterans of Foreign Wars (VFW) used it as a social hall and meeting hall. The VFW moved out in 1979, and the building slowly deteriorated. In 1981, the National Park Service declared the Beach Chalet a National Landmark because of the important frescoes, mosaics, and woodcarvings now visible in the ground-floor visitor center. Despite the declaration, however, the building remained unused for another fifteen years, until one day Sunset residents Lara and Gar Truppelli saw a "for lease" sign. Gar was in his last semester at San Francisco State and needed to write a business plan for his final assignment.

The duo were also home brewers, and they thought the location was ideal for their dream restaurant and pub. Lara recalls that their "market research" was marching up and down the beach and

The murals inside the visitor center were created in the 1930s and depict scenes from everyday life in San Francisco.

Left: A table with a view of Ocean Beach. Photo courtesy of Beach Chalet

Center: Gar and Lara Truppelli. Photo courtesy of Beach Chalet

Right: Check out the ground floor visitor center and murals. Photo courtesy of Kimberley Lovato

neighborhood streets asking surfers and residents what they would like in a local restaurant. The proposal was submitted, and though Lara says they knew it was a long shot because of their youth and inexperience, the city accepted. Lara guesses it was their vision for revitalizing the historic waterfront building as a place for everyone that sealed the deal. Beach Chalet reopened in 1996 with a line out the front door and has been packing people in ever since.

Upstairs, above the visitor center, is Beach Chalet Restaurant, where you can grab fresh catch or steaks served with a heavenly view of the beach and the Pacific. Downstairs, behind the visitor center, is the sunny Park Chalet, where burgers and fish and chips can be eaten while listening to live music on weekends, or while sitting in the garden sipping the homemade brews, whose names (VFW Golden Ale, California Kind, and Riptide Red) nod to the history of the oceanfront building, as well as the handiwork of two students with a big dream.

1000 Great Hwy.
415-386-8439
www.beachchalet.com
Neighborhood: Outer Sunset

BELCAMPO

A conscientious carnivore

When you're curious about how to get access to better food, farming is the natural place to start. At least it was for Anya Fernald, the cofounder of Belcampo, a meat empire born in 2012 with 6,000 acres and a vision of raising animals in an organic, sustainable, and compassionate way. Today her grass-fed and pasture-raised cattle, sheep, and pigs live on a 20,000-acre farm near Mt. Shasta. The farm is certified both humane and 100 percent organic. Belcampo also has its own slaughterhouse, as well as an e-commerce platform and a handful of butcher shop-restaurants, including the corner gem on Polk Street.

Anya's love of meat was validated while living for six years in the Piedmont region of Italy, where eating salami or raw beef as a starter to almost every meal was the norm. When Anya arrived home in 2006, she says it was hard to find the same high quality, so she started buying whole cows from a local farmer and learned how to butcher meat. Her professional resume includes time at Slow Food Italy and Slow Food Nations. She founded the Food Craft Institute and the Eat Real Fest in Oakland and has appeared as a judge on the Food Network's *Iron Chef America*. It was when Anya started a consulting firm that a client, Todd Robinson, approached her with the opportunity to cocreate a vertically integrated,

> "Going to the butcher should include a little relaxation, some nice conversation, and you should feel great about your choices."
> ~Anya Fernald

Top left: Anya Fernald is the founder of Belcampo Meat Co. and farm. Photo courtesy of Belcampo Meat Co.

Top right: A Belcampo table setting at the Russian Hill restaurant. Photo courtesy of Belcampo Meat Co.

Above left: Belcampo's Russian Hill butcher shop is a neighborhood favorite. Photo courtesy of Belcampo Meat Co.

Above right: Belcampo's restaurant is behind the butcher shop and serves fresh food from the farm. Photo courtesy of Belcampo Meat Co.

sustainable, and profitable food business. The butcher shop carries meat exclusively from Belcampo's farm. You can buy steaks, ground beef, chops, and salami and ask questions about the philosophy of transparency and minimal waste. The restaurant's burger-focused menu (the Double Fast Burger is Anya's favorite) satisfies other conscientious carnivores.

1998 Polk St.
415-660-5573
www.belcampo.com
Neighborhood: Russian Hill

BI-RITE MARKET

Community-minded market

Everyone loves a neighborhood bodega, and Bi-Rite Market in the Mission was, and still is, a favorite. It was first run by a family in 1940, then taken over by brothers Ned and Jack Mogannam, Palestinian immigrants who bought the market in 1964. Ned's sons, Sam and Raphael, spent their childhood weekends and summers stocking shelves.

Little did they know that twenty-six years later they'd be at the helm of a market—and a movement. Ned and Jack sold the store in 1987 to an independent operator, and the local vibe and fresh ingredients all but withered away until 1997, when Sam and Raphael brought Bi-Rite back into the family. Sam went through a period of eschewing the family business and, like most kids, wanted to blaze a new trail. He says he always wanted to feed people, and as the chef/owner of now-closed Rendezvous du Monde restaurant in San Francisco's Financial District, he did that for a while. But the lure of the family memories and legacy, and the encouragement of his father, pulled him back to Bi-Rite. Sam says he thought about a new name, too, but kept it after he saw the now iconic Art Deco Bi-Rite sign in a book called *Deco by the Bay* by Michael Crowe.

What he did change, however, was the store's approach to food. Sam's experience as a chef means customers get a dose of hospitality

Check out the Bi-Rite Creamery ice cream shop down the street.

Left: Bi-Rite Market has been a Mission District favorite since 1940. Photo courtesy of Kimberley Lovato

Right: Sam Mogannam. Photo courtesy of Bi-Rite Market

not found in large grocery stores and shelves filled with high-quality, local ingredients. Spend any time in front of the overflowing bins of plump fruit and crisp vegetables grown on Bi-Rite's farm in Sonoma, or at the deli counter where wholesome food is prepared daily in the commercial kitchen, and Sam's high standards are palpable. But Bi-Rite is more than just what's inside its walls. It is also a hub of activism, deeply rooted in promoting good and healthy eating, especially through its 18 Reasons education center, where cooking classes, school nutrition programs, and other sustainability-minded initiatives simmer and blend, proving that a neighborhood grocery store can not only feed people but also nourish a community.

3639 Eighteenth St.
415-241-9760
www.biritemarket.com
Neighborhood: Mission

BLUE PLATE

The no-plan plan

What happens when some college buddies buy four chandeliers at a flea market and joke about how good they would look hanging in a restaurant? They buy a restaurant to hang them in, of course. Jeff Trenam and Cory Obenour opened Blue Plate in 1999, and more than seventeen years later the unassuming place with the neon blue sign is a beloved neighborhood mainstay in the Outer Mission. Jeff can hardly believe it himself, thinking about the initial plan, which he says was basically to have a place where they could hang out together, show off the art of their creative buddies, and party. Ah, youth.

It turns out the plan wasn't half bad. Jeff says working with his coworkers and friends makes it feel like a party every night, and when you like what you do, that spreads and grows into a lifestyle. San Francisco has changed a lot since Blue Plate opened, ushering in Michelin stars and star chefs, but Jeff says Blue Plate is still that local place where anyone can come sit at the counter and never feel alone. Three cozy, interconnected rooms spread across the old Victorian house that belies the restaurant's basic facade, and it's not uncommon to see families celebrating graduations over plates of fried chicken, meatloaf, or pork osso buco, or a birthday candle flickering in a slice of key lime pie.

> "We talk a lot about food sustainability but not enough about cultural sustainability, the process of slowing down and sharing a meal with someone."
> ~Jeff Trenam

Left: Blue Plate is a neighborhood favorite. Photo courtesy of Blue Plate

Right: Jeff Trenam greets guests with a smile on a busy Saturday night. Photo courtesy of Kimberley Lovato

Things are more focused now, says Jeff. The menu has evolved, too, and there is an easy sophistication to each dish. "It's still familiar and still no fuss, but with a fine-tuned execution," says Jeff. And those four chandeliers? Yep, still hanging around along with the good friends and artists—almost as if it were planned that way.

3218 Mission St.
415-282-6777
www.blueplatesf.com
Neighborhood: Outer Mission/Bernal Heights

BOB'S DONUTS

Where old school is cool

While doughnut shops have gone glam across the country, Bob's is still a bastion of linoleum counters and fluorescent lights that wears its retro style like it's the latest trend. This family-run joint has fueled morning coffee breaks and post-late-night drinking binges since opening in the 1960s, making fresh pastries and doughnuts twenty-four hours a day, seven days a week. It is one of San Francisco's last independent doughnut shops, and faces press against the glass window facing Polk Street, drooling over usual suspects such as glazed, chocolate, sprinkles, and sugar. But things get downright lustful when there are fresh apple fritters or crumb- or custard-filled doughnuts in the window. Feeling extra gluttonous? Take Bob's Giant Donut Challenge, a gut-busting dare to finish the larger-than-your-head doughnut within three minutes. If you succeed, you'll get your money back, a Bob's Donuts t-shirt, and gloating rights as your name is penned onto the Hall of Fame. The stomachache is a bonus.

1621 Polk St.
415-776-3141
www.bobsdonutssf.com
Neighborhood: Polk Gulch

Follow @whatsfreshest on Twitter and @bobsdonuts on Instagram for fresh-from-the-fryer pictures.

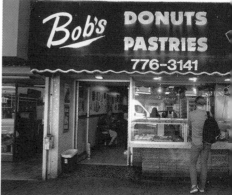

Top right: Bob's is beloved for its old-school atmosphere and 24/7 access to doughnuts. Photo courtesy of Kimberley Lovato

Above left: This supersized belly buster is what Bob's Donut Challenge legends are made of. Photo courtesy of Kimberley Lovato

Above right: Bob's has been a Polk Street pit stop since opening in the 1960s. Photo courtesy of Kimberley Lovato

BRAINWASH CAFE & LAUNDROMAT

Fluff, fold, food

Caffeine, food, Wi-Fi, and laundry all under one roof? No, you are not at Mom's house. It's BrainWash, the brainchild of Susan Schindler, a businesswoman who was in the market for a location to open a nightclub. After discovering there was no laundromat in SoMa, a light bulb went on, and she created the coolest one around.

That was thirty years ago, and rumors have swirled that BrainWash got its name because it was located across the street from the building where Patty Hearst was held captive in 1974. That's just spin-cycle gossip. The real story has a little less intrigue. Susan had the epiphany while clipping coupons for laundry detergent. She eventually sold BrainWash in 1999 to current owner Jeff Zalles, who had been in the laundry business in New York and says he fell in love with the concept of a laundromat gathering spot. BrainWash has coin-operated machines, dry cleaning, and fluff-and-fold service.

Most of his customers are from the neighborhood, and he says plenty of laundry has been left over the years because people simply forget they've come to do a tedious chore. Hanging out at BrainWash feels far from that. The walls are decked with paintings

> "Doing laundry is a little cooler here."
> ~Jeff Zalles

Top right: Doing laundry has never been so much fun. Photo courtesy of Kimberley Lovato

Above left: Wash, dry, fold, eat, repeat. Photo courtesy of Kimberley Lovato

Above right: Drink and eat while your delicates dry. Photo courtesy of Kimberley Lovato

from local artists. The kitchen opens early for made-to-order breakfast, lunch, and dinner (all available for takeout), and you can get cheap beer at happy hour, between 4 p.m. and 7 p.m. every day. Jeff also manages a calendar of live music and stand-up comedy acts every night of the week. Washing clothes while laughing your socks off? It's an atmosphere worth soaking in, if only until your delicates are dry.

1122 Folsom St.
415-861-3663
www.brainwash.com
Neighborhood: SoMa

THE BRAZEN HEAD

Finders keepers

If you blink, you'll walk right by The Brazen Head. Not because it's tiny but because there is no sign announcing you've landed on the doorstep of a neighborhood pub where comfort food, good drinks, and discretion have been on tap for more than thirty-five years.

Despite the missing identifier, former San Francisco 49er Steve Young, New York Yankee Derek Jeter, and even Mick Jagger of the Rolling Stones found the place. It seems it was a lucky find for owner Eddie Savino, too. He arrived in San Francisco from the Bronx in July 1979 with a hundred dollars in his pocket, a couch to sleep on, and every intention of returning home. Instead he landed a job at nearby Liverpool Lil's.

A few years later he moved over to The Brazen Head, where he worked for eleven years before purchasing it in 1993. No surprise—a few things have changed. "The '80s in San Francisco had no rules. Everyone was swinging for the fences on most nights. The social scene is much calmer now. It's also so much more expensive to live here, which brings a different personality," says Eddie. Opened in 1980, the time-capsule tavern serves better-than-average pub grub, such as pepper New York steak, prime rib, filet mignon, double-cut pork chops, and French onion soup.

> "What happens in the dimly lit Brazen Head stays in The Brazen Head. We pride ourselves on discretion and enjoy the intimate behavior that brings."
> ~Eddie Savino

Top: Blink and you might walk right by this beloved pub-resto. Photo courtesy of Bea D'Amico

Above left: Locals gather for good food and a belly up to the bar. Photo courtesy of Bea D'Amico

Above right: Wood-paneled walls and comfort food make this a cozy favorite. Photo courtesy of Bea D'Amico

But what really brings people in again and again, he says, is the staff, many of whom have been Brazen Heads for double-digit years and have longstanding relationships with customers. One employee Eddie remembers well is Marcella, whom he hired in 1985. The two have been married for twenty-seven years now. Whether it's via word of mouth, a local referral, or from reading a fabulous guidebook (like this one), once you find The Brazen Head, you will soon see why locals prefer to keep it a secret.

3166 Buchanan St.
415-921-7600
www.brazenheadsf.com
Neighborhood: Cow Hollow

BREAKFAST AT TIFFANY'S

It takes a neighborhood

Greasy spoon, coffee shop, dive—whatever you call it, the great American diner is often a ketchup-splotched nexus of neighborhood meet-ups, gossip sessions, and local news, and there's no exception when it comes to this Portola gem. Former owner Gerald "Gerry" Adan had run the diner since 1978. When he passed away in 2013, a businessman named Kash Feng bought the building as an investment, planning to turn the diner into a dumpling den. Though he has lived in the neighborhood for fifteen years, he says he wasn't a regular at Breakfast at Tiffany's.

No sooner had he taken possession than neighbors started to pop in and inquire about when Breakfast at Tiffany's would reopen. The Portola Neighborhood Association contacted Kash, too, imploring him to reconsider his dumpling-in-place-of-the-diner plan. Even the City of San Francisco got involved and offered Kash some cash.

He says there was no way he could get rid of Breakfast at Tiffany's. The overwhelming neighborhood support showed him that keeping it was the only thing to do. Kash gussied things up and modernized the kitchen, but the old-timey diner vibe stayed, with its swivel counter stools, free coffee refills, and specials written on a chalkboard that belonged to Gerry.

> Breakfast at Tiffany's was named for Gerry's niece, Tiffany.
> Sorry, Audrey Hepburn fans.

Top left: Breakfast at Tiffany's window sign. Photo courtesy of Michael Ogata

Top right: Old photos deck the walls. Photo courtesy of Michael Ogata

Above left: A trio of corned beef, fried chicken, and hash-brown Benedict. Photo courtesy of Michael Ogata

Above right: The corner neighborhood diner is a local favorite. Photo courtesy of Michael Ogata

On reopening day there was a line out the door, and business has been business-as-usual ever since. Regulars come in at their regular times, and former chef Dennis Baca returned to the kitchen, dishing out pancakes, omelets, hash browns, eggs Benedict, biscuits and gravy, and tater tot skillets. Kash says he has absolutely no regrets. "I love going in there," he says, "because everyone is so happy."

2499 San Bruno Ave.
415-468-8805
www.breakfastattiffanyssf.com
Neighborhood: Portola

BRENDA'S FRENCH SOUL FOOD

Southern comfort

B renda Buenviaje didn't plan to be a chef, but she always had good food in her midst. That happens when your childhood outside of New Orleans includes fishing off the family's boat, crabbing in the bayous, and picking pecans and berries in a land where Cajun, Creole, and crawfish are the three C's of a Louisiana upbringing. Brenda planned to be an artist, and after graduating from LSU she settled into studio life, where hours of painting spilled into weeks and months.

To break up the monotony, Brenda read books. Not just any old books—cookbooks. The first one she remembers having a real impact on her was Jeff Smith's *The Frugal Gourmet Cooks Three Ancient Cuisines: China, Greece, and Rome,* which Brenda says she loved for its combined education of food, geography, and history. She cooked from it, too. When not painting or trying out new recipes, Brenda worked at an art supply store, where her colleagues eventually suggested a career in cooking because it was all she talked about. Jump ahead to 2017 and Brenda's resume counts kitchens in New Orleans, Denver, and San Francisco. She opened Brenda's French Soul Food with a plan to satiate this city's mad love for French fare, but with a dash of her NOLA roots on the side. She says it wasn't long after Hurricane Katrina devastated her home state when a lot of Louisianans began turning up at the restaurant in search of authentic shrimp and grits,

> Brenda's signature crawfish beignets have become a cult classic.

Top: Restaurant interior. Photo courtesy of Libby Truesdell

Above left: Exterior. Photo courtesy of Libby Truesdell

Above center: Brenda brings her Cajun soul to San Francisco. Photo courtesy of Libby Truesdell

Above right: Fried chicken. Photo courtesy of Libby Truesdell

muffuletta sandwiches, oyster po'boys, and beignets. Brenda says cooking is not far off from creating art. You're still working to appease the critics, but the difference, she says, is in the return on the investment. "With oil paintings it can take years to finish and get it hung in a gallery, whereas cooking gets immediate face-to-face feedback."

Judging from the lineup of smiling regulars spilling out the front door, the critics are hungry and satisfied.

652 Polk St.
415-345-8100
www.frenchsoulfood.com
Neighborhood: Tenderloin

THE BUENA VISTA

Irish coffee, San Francisco-style

A Pulitzer Prize-winning writer walks into a bar. It sounds like the beginning of a joke, but it actually happened in San Francisco on November 10, 1952. The scribe was Stanton Delaplane, a longtime columnist for the *San Francisco Chronicle*, and the bar was the Buena Vista, opened in 1916 as a boarding house and then converted to a saloon and hangout for local fishermen. But it wasn't until Stanton sauntered in and regaled then-bar owner Jack Koeppler with accounts of a smooth whiskey and coffee drink he had quaffed at the airport in Shannon, Ireland, that a local legend was born.

Thinking fog-cloaked San Francisco was the ideal place for the warm beverage, Jack challenged Stanton to help recreate the coffee drink he'd encountered on the Emerald Isle. The oft-told story goes that Stanton agreed, and the two men spent the night measuring, pouring, stirring, and sipping, but the taste was a little off. More worrisome, the signature thick cuff of cream that crowned the coffee-whiskey blend sank like a Blarney stone. Undeterred, Jack not only made a trek to Shannon Airport to find his muse, but also consulted a prominent San Francisco dairy owner, who revealed that heavy cream, slightly frothed, would float like a cloud. Flash forward seven decades, and the Buena Vista's Irish coffee is as much a San Francisco specialty as the damp and foggy days it was intended to rebuff.

The BV serves around two thousand Irish coffees per day.

Left: In 1954, the first shipment of Tullamore Dew whiskey arrives in San Francisco. Photo courtesy of The Buena Vista

Center: It's 1956, and The Buena Vista is hopping, with trays of Irish coffee being served. Photo courtesy of The Buena Vista

Right: The bartenders at The Buena Vista add a frothy cap of cream to each Irish coffee. Photo courtesy of The Buena Vista

   To locals, the bar-restaurant is the BV, and there is often a line at the door before opening. Luckily, the view of the city's famed cable cars chugging down the Hyde Street hill is almost as entertaining as the real show inside. BV bartenders in crisp white coats line up water-heated glass goblets on the wooden bar, drop in two cubes of sugar, and pour in the coffee, followed by a jigger of Tullamore Dew Irish whiskey, and finally float that essential rim of whipped white cream on top, all faster than you can order the second one, which, according to longtime bartender Joseph, is always better than the first. True or false? There's only one way to find out.

2765 Hyde St.
415-474-5044
www.thebuenavista.com
Neighborhood: Fisherman's Wharf

BURMA SUPERSTAR

Baby, I'm a star

When Desmond Tan emigrated from Burma to San Francisco in 1977, he was only eleven years old and could not have known that he would one day own the Richmond District restaurant he and his family frequented on special occasions and which was his go-to spot for mohinga, a noodle and fish soup that's practically the national dish of Burma. One day in 2001, Desmond learned that the family that owned Burma Superstar was planning on selling the restaurant. Knowing what he had to do to secure his mohinga connection, Desmond says he went from tech entrepreneur to restaurateur within twenty-four hours.

He revamped the haphazard menu that he says was a mash-up of Americanized Chinese and Burmese dishes and incorporated more authentic flavors, such as fish sauce and tamarind. Burmese cooking takes a lot of its influence from neighboring China, India, Thailand, and Laos, and Desmond's menu now includes curries, noodle dishes, and stews. But it's the way the ingredients are combined and their texture that makes Burmese food stand out. That's why garlic, onion, nuts, seeds, shallots, and yellow split peas are fried into crispy bits that add oomph to soups and salads.

Speaking of salads—mention Burma Superstar in San Francisco and the Pavlovian response might be "tea leaf salad." The legendary

> "To many, Burma is still mysterious, so Burma Superstar is a way to unveil a seemingly distant culture."
> ~Desmond Tan

Top left: Burma Superstar's tea leaf salad. Photo courtesy of Burma Superstar

Top right: Burma Superstar on a quiet weekday. Photo courtesy of Bea D'Amico

Above: Waiting is normal at Burma Superstar. Photo courtesy of Burma Superstar

dish is mixed tableside and is one of the most popular dishes on the menu. Legendary, too, are the wait times at the no-reservations spot. To help ease the pain a little, Desmond recently cowrote and released a cookbook with Kate Leahy, *Burma Superstar: Addictive Recipes from the Crossroads of Southeast Asia,* that includes ninety recipes he hopes will transcend borders and bring the flavors of his home to yours.

309 Clement St.
415-387-2147
www.burmasuperstar.com
Neighborhood: Richmond

CAFE ZOETROPE

Coppola's café

Wedged like a slice of green pie between North Beach and Chinatown, the historic Sentinel Building, a.k.a. Columbus Tower, stands out not only for its flatiron style but also for the notable tenants who have wandered its halls over the years, and still do. The Grateful Dead recorded *Anthem of the Sun* in the building, and the Kingston Trio once owned it and sold it to the current owner, famed director Francis Ford Coppola, who set up American Zoetrope film studio here in 1972. A few films you might have heard of, including *The Godfather II* and *III* and *Apocalypse Now*, were written, edited, or sound mixed within these walls. The studio's namesake café is filled with family photos, movie posters, personal artwork, and career mementos.

It's a place where you'll find patrons talking to one another rather than texting, and reading the newspapers instead of computer screens. The tiny bar pours Francis Ford Coppola wine, and the menu features some Coppola family recipes, including the director's own veal, beef, and pork meatballs. Snapping photos of the roped-off corner booth is allowed, but it is reserved for family members (though you could nab it last minute on a busy night). And yes, the famous producer-director does stop in occasionally.

916 Kearny St.
415-291-1700
www.cafecoppola.com
Neighborhood: North Beach

Top left: The Coppola family booth is roped off in case they drop by, but it sometimes opens up to patrons. Photo courtesy of Kimberley Lovato

Above left: The restaurant walls are decked with movie memorabilia that pays homage to Coppola's illustrious career. Photo courtesy of Kimberley Lovato

Above right: The cozy bar is a casual meeting spot. Photo courtesy of Kimberley Lovato

CALA

A fresh take

Cala is not your average Mexican restaurant, and despite San Francisco's passion for south-of-the-border cuisine, that's a good thing. Cala is owned by Gabriela Cámara of Mexico City's lauded Contramar, which she says she opened primarily as a result of trips to the beach. "You get beautiful seafood there that was prepared simply right on the beach, and that kind of food wasn't really available in Mexico City. There wasn't a place for fresh, traditional preparations of Mexican seafood," she says. Cala is San Francisco's take on the Mexico City institution, with a menu that also salutes the sea and California bounty.

Though simple in its list of ingredients, the sophisticated menu marries light and fresh flavors, mostly vegetarian and seafood, in an unusual enough way that you hardly notice the absent pork, chicken, or beef enchiladas smothered in red sauce. Served tapas style, the dishes arrive in a conga-line succession of delicious bites, easy for sharing. The trout tostadas with avocado, chipotle mayonnaise, and crispy leeks are a fan favorite, as are the charred sweet potato with bone-marrow salsa negra and vegetarian-friendly sopes playeros with black beans, crema, and ricotta salata.

When Gabriela isn't in San Francisco, she relies on her creative team, including chef de cuisine Kenny Curran, whom she calls "a talented artist with impeccable taste." Cala opened in 2015 in a

In the alley behind the restaurant, Tacos Cala serves Mexico City-style tacos de guisado (braised vegetable and/or meat dishes) with homemade corn tortillas every day from 11 to 2.

Top left: Cala's bright dining room packs them in. Photo courtesy of Cala

Top right: Cala's simple exterior belies the vibrancy of the menu. Photo courtesy of Chloe List

Above left: Cala's taco stand, behind the restaurant. Photo courtesy of Chloe List

Above center: Gabriela Cámara. Photo courtesy of Yvonne Venegas

Above right: Trout tostada with chipotle, avocado, and fried leeks. Photo courtesy of Chloe List

former parking garage, and its whitewashed, concrete walls, high ceilings, and floods of natural light give it that urban-meets-the-beach feel reminiscent of Gabriela's Mexico City institution. Cala is her first foray into the United States, and she says a combination of factors brought her here, mainly opportunity and timing.

The hardest part of opening in San Francisco, however, was staffing a restaurant full of people who can afford to live in the same city where they work. To that end Cala adds 20 percent to all bills and offers full benefits to its employees. The tab might be higher because of it, but it's another fresh take worth savoring nonetheless.

149 Fell St.
415-660-7701
www.calarestaurant.com
Neighborhood: Hayes Valley

THE CANDY STORE

The sweet life

There's nothing like saltwater taffy, Pop Rocks, or a hand-swirled lollipop as big as your head to transport you to a day at the beachside boardwalk or a log cabin at summer camp. This feeling is summoned each time you step into the pristine Candy Store and see the glass jars, full of chewy, gummy, and crunchy candies in a rainbow of colors, lining the wall. The shop, which opened in 2007, was the perfect prescription for owner Diane Campbell, who'd dreamed of her own sugarcoated shop since she was a young girl in Great Neck, Long Island. She recalls a neighborhood spot called, not coincidentally, the Candy Store. It was where kids gathered on weekends and spent their allowances. Unfortunately for Diane, candy was forbidden in her house, but like any kid faced with a candy embargo, she found another way—the neighborhood ice cream man, who sold her candy lipsticks, Fun Dip, and Zotz.

At ten, Diane began peddling bags of gummy bears from her locker, calling herself the richest girl in school. Though she's had many jobs since then, the idea of running her own candy store stuck. Eventually she and her husband found their way to San Francisco. The Candy Store, just like her childhood neighborhood haunt, stocks old-time favorites such as Abba-Zaba bars, wax bottles, and Pixy Stix, as well as some local chocolate and rare confections from

> The "Blast From The Past" gift box assembles old-school favorites and can be ordered online.

Top right: Diane Campbell is living her childhood candy store dream. Photo courtesy of Kimberley Lovato

Above left: A neighborhood sweet spot. Photo courtesy of Kimberley Lovato

Above right: Many of the candies are imported from Europe. Photo courtesy of Kimberley Lovato

around the world. She's been open for ten years now, and on any given day a steady stream of candy lovers stops in to taste what's new, order gifts, or just say hi. Diane greets them by name and plops sweets in the open hands of kids who look about the same age as Diane must have been when The Candy Store idea was born, their eyes wide with sugary dreams.

1507 Vallejo St.
415-921-8000
www.thecandystoresf.com
Neighborhood: Russian Hill

THE CHEESE SCHOOL OF SAN FRANCISCO

Say cheese

You're not alone if you point to the oblong sign dangling over the sidewalk and say, "There's a cheese school in San Francisco?" Owner Kiri Fisher says it happens all the time. That America's only independent cheese school is located right here in San Francisco is as much of a surprise to some locals as opening a cheese school was to Kiri. When the former publisher folded her magazine, she says she had one thought that calmed her nerves—a vision of what she wanted to do next: find an open field, hang out with sheep for a while, and make cheese. The idea of working with her hands also appealed.

After a few cheesemaking internships and counter jobs, Kiri joined the California Artisan Cheese Festival working with instructors and organizing classes, which resonated with her. After meeting cheesemongers and farmers, she appreciated the dedication, tradition, and hard work behind cheesemaking and knew she didn't want to do it herself. The Cheese School of San Francisco was born in 2011 from a cheese shop in North Beach that offered classes on the side. Through the gossip mill, or perhaps the cheese shredder, Kiri learned the business was for sale and bought it with partner Daphne Zepos, an educator, cheesemaker, importer, and one of the most respected authorities on cheese in America, who sadly passed away a year later.

> "I don't know of a lot of other places outside of San Francisco where you could do this."
> ~Kiri Fisher

Top left: Kiri Fisher, owner of The Cheese School of San Francisco. Photo courtesy of Kiri Fisher

Top right: A classroom at The Cheese School of San Francisco. Photo courtesy of Kiri Fisher

Above left: Yes, there is a cheese school in San Francisco. Photo courtesy of Kiri Fisher

Above right: Getting ready to learn all about cheese at The Cheese School of San Francisco. Photo courtesy of Kiri Fisher

The school eventually moved to its current location in the Mission and offers a slew of classes, including Cheese 101, which Kiri usually teaches herself, and the most popular: making mozzarella, burrata, and ricotta. Daphne had started a master class series that provided continuing education for cheesemongers and other professionals, which continues today. But the best part of running a cheese school for Kiri? The delight she sees in people when they try something new, or when they discover there is so much to know and learn about cheese. And, she admits, she does enjoy watching people point at the sign of the funny little business in San Francisco that started with a vision of a field of sheep.

2124 Folsom St.
415-346-7530
www.thecheeseschool.com
Neighborhood: Mission

CHINA LIVE

The Chinese cuisine scene

If you like themed food halls like New York's Eataly, then you'll adore China Live, San Francisco's 30,000-square-foot ode to Chinese cuisine.

Created by well-known San Francisco restaurateur and chef George Chen of Betelnut (R.I.P.) fame, China Live is his personal mission to change the way we think about Chinese food. George says he hopes to eliminate the preconceived notions of it being a cheap and unhealthy cuisine by spotlighting the fresh-ingredient-driven ethos that has always been at the core of cooking in China.

After years of creation and renovation, China Live's modern interior centers on the ground floor Market Restaurant, with a bar, tea lounge, and café with daily changing menus of Chinese regional specialties prepared in open kitchens. Choose from dumplings, stir fry, rice and noodles, fresh seafood, Chinese charcuterie and barbecue, and other delights. Diners are treated to up-close views of cooking styles and demonstrations, including the rare wa guan tang, a giant ceramic slow cooker used for many Chinese recipes.

Upstairs, and only accessible via a back-alley entrance, the upscale Eight Tables by George Chen features an ever-evolving eight-course tasting menu. "It's time Chinese food takes its place among the world's great cuisines, and Eight Tables will push Chinese

The retail shop sells condiments, spices, cookware, and gifts hand selected from China.

Top right: Oolong Café within China Live. Photo courtesy of China Live

Above left: George Chen, cofounder of China Live. Photo courtesy of China Live

Above right: The retail space sells high-quality Chinese products. Photo courtesy of Patricia Chang

gastronomy to new heights," he says. There is also a luxurious lounge with views of Chinatown, evoking old Shanghai and serving a lot of single malt Scotch-based cocktails. Eventually there will be a rooftop bar—the cherry on top of a place that lives up to its "variety is the spice of dining life" maxim.

644 Broadway
415-788-8188
www.chinalivesf.com
Neighborhood: Chinatown

CINDERELLA RUSSIAN BAKERY & CAFÉ

From Russia, with love

Though it has a fairytale name, there is nothing make believe about this authentic Russian bakery and café that has been satisfying piroshki and cabbage roll cravings since 1953.

When Mike Fishman landed in the city in 1988 from the Soviet Union, it wasn't long before the tight-knit Russian community pointed him toward Cinderella. He recalls that two Russian women ran the bakery, and when they decided to retire years later, Mike seized the opportunity to continue business. Though Mike had been in the food business in Russia, the two women trained him for months, he says, passing on their recipes and knowledge. Mike and his wife became the sole owners in 2008 and changed the look of the place from dated diner to cozy café and bakery. They also expanded the kitchen and added a smattering of tables out front. Mike made some adjustments to the menu, too, focusing on high-quality ingredients to create his made-from-scratch baked goods and food every day.

His customers are both Russians and San Franciscans who, Mike says, value diversity and learning about different cultures through food such as piroshki, small turnovers with sweet or savory fillings; pelmeni, boiled meat dumplings; and Siberian-style meat pies.

> Cinderella is the oldest homestyle
> Russian bakery in the Bay Area.

Top right: Cinderella has been in San Francisco since 1953. Photo courtesy of Kimberley Lovato

Above left: Mike Fishman came to the US from Russia in 1988. Photo courtesy of Kimberley Lovato

Above right: Russian specialties are made fresh daily. Photo courtesy of Kimberley Lovato

Cold, foggy days are great for borscht, a ruby-red beet soup served steaming hot with sour cream and fresh dill. Come Easter, Cinderella makes paskha, a molded cheesecake-like dessert, and kulich, an Easter bread with raisins and candied orange peel. Happily ever after at Cinderella, however, is found in a loaf of bread—Mike's dark and chewy rye bread, to be exact. Made from a recipe he brought with him from Russia, it's divine slathered with butter or dipped in a bowl of Babushka's chicken soup. "It tastes of childhood," says Mike.

436 Balboa St.
415-751-9690
www.cinderellabakery.com
Neighborhood: Inner Richmond

CIOPPINO

San Francisco's stew

Let's get this out of the way now—cioppino is pronounced chuh-PEE-no, and this tomato-based seafood stew takes its name from the word *ciuppin*, a word that means "little soup" in the Genoese dialect. Italian fishermen who arrived in San Francisco in the late 1800s would dump their leftover catch into pots and cook it. Over time, chefs spiced it up with garlic, onions, herbs, and wine, along with clams, shrimp, mussels, and local Dungeness crab, transforming it into San Francisco's signature dish.

You'll find fantastic versions around the city, each using certain kinds of seafood, a pinch of saffron, or a zing of chili to make it stand out from the rest. But everyone agrees that it is not cioppino without a loaf of crunchy San Francisco sourdough bread to sop up the broth and a bib to catch the splatter.

Try it.

Cioppino's on Fisherman's Wharf is named for the stew for good reason.

400 Jefferson St.
415-775-9311
cioppinos.letseat.at

Sotto Mare in North Beach is always packed thanks to its "best damn crab cioppino."

552 Green St.
415-398-3181
www.sottomaresf.com

The cioppino is so good at Cioppino's, they named their restaurant after it. Photo courtesy of Cioppino's

Tadich Grill serves more than 22,000 bowls a year.

240 California St.
415-391-1849
www.tadichgrill.com

Counter culture

When Woolworth's closed the last of its lovable five-and-dime stores in 1997, including the bustling downtown San Francisco branch at Powell and Market Streets, gone with them went a mayonnaise-slathered slice of dining history—the luncheonette. These counters hemmed into the backs of variety stores fed egg-salad and BLT sandwiches, lemonade, and root-beer floats to generations of families and shoppers.

Leave it to a San Francisco native to style up the idea for a new age. "My mom and grandmother and I used to frequent lunch counters in Miami, places like Allen's Drugs on Red Road and Sunset Drugs, all of those old lunch counters in drugstores that were so fun. They were all very Deco and provided much of the inspiration for City Counter," says founder Harper Matheson, who opened City Counter at the bottom of the Standard Oil Building in May 2017.

Open from lunch through happy hour (yes, this modern luncheonette serves California wine and beer), City Counter hearkens back to old-school luncheonettes without the kitsch of a theme restaurant. The all-white diner and thirty-seat counter is monochrome sleek, while a pink, neon "C" adds Deco zing. But the real focus, says Harper, is on quick food for busy downtowners that's good enough to, well, eat. Consulting chef Sean Thomas of Blue

Come for happy hour counter snacks, such as salt-and-vinegar popcorn, salt cod deviled eggs, and classic potato chips.

Top left: A fresh take on an old classic. Photo courtesy of City Counter

Top right: A gooey and good grilled cheese is always a good idea. Photo courtesy of Kassie Borreson

Above left: Grab a place at the counter. Photo courtesy of Kassie Borreson

Above right: Harper Matheson, founder of City Counter. Photo courtesy of Kassie Borreson

Plate puts a sophisticated slant on familiar luncheonette sandwiches, such as the "Reuben-esque," a vegetarian take on a classic with smoked beets instead of corned beef. The deviled egg salad has crushed salt-and-vinegar chips mixed right in. There is a classic club sandwich and a tuna melt made with a three-cheese fondue. You can count on fresh pie or a root-beer float for dessert. Four huge bay windows invite hurried passersby to peek in at an old tradition making a comeback (hopefully) in downtown San Francisco.

115 Sansome St.
415-844-0633
www.citycountersf.com
Neighborhood: Financial District

CLIFF HOUSE

History with a view

Like a phoenix, the Cliff House has risen from the ashes several times over its 154-year life. Built in 1893 on a precipice overlooking the Pacific Ocean, the single-story roadhouse was a dining and dancing destination by the sea for the wealthy, who traveled by horseback along Point Lobos Road, now Geary Boulevard, from downtown San Francisco.

Search for historic photos of the Cliff House and you'll likely see the eight-story Victorian castle built by Adolph Sutro, a self-made millionaire, philanthropist, and later mayor of San Francisco, who bought the Cliff House from its original owners. The grand building survived the 1906 earthquake but burned down shortly thereafter, as had its predecessor. During the more than one hundred years since then, the Cliff House has outwitted ocean storms, earthquakes, the Sutro Baths fire, more owners and renovations, Prohibition and the Great Depression, and government shutdowns.

The grande dame is nothing if not a survivor. But she'd become dowdy, and the food was no longer a draw. Mary and Dan Hountalas took over ownership in 1973 (the National Park Service bought the Cliff House in 1977, keeping Mary and Dan on as concessionaires) and hired chef Kevin Weber to revamp the menu. The Hountalas family has been a part of the Ocean Beach community since 1906, and Dan recalls diving for crabs near the Cliff House with his father.

The Cliff House holds a popular Sunday champagne brunch.

Top: The eight-story Victorian version of the Cliff House burned down shortly after the 1906 earthquake. Photo courtesy of Cliff House

Above left: The Cliff House Bistro is a casual spot with stellar sea views. Photo courtesy of Kimberley Lovato

Above right: Cliff House chef Kevin Weber. Photo courtesy of Cliff House

They say they are honored to be a part of breathing new life into the landmark and making it a destination again, as it was before the turn of the century. Thanks to their chef, Kevin, food is no longer an afterthought. He's been at the Cliff House now for more than forty years, and he oversees the menus of the casual walk-in bistro and the more upscale Sutro's Restaurant. Kevin pulls the signature popovers hot from the oven every twenty minutes. The bloody Marys are popular, and the Cliff House Dungeness Crab Louis Salad is a mainstay. Though many might think of the Cliff House as a tourists-only restaurant, Dan confirms that 80 percent of his guests are locals, many from the surrounding neighborhood and farther afield who remember it when and return to reminisce about the jewel on the cliff that sparkles anew.

1090 Point Lobos Ave.
415-386-3330
www.cliffhouse.com
Neighborhood: Sea Cliff

Top: Cliff House has a long and storied history. Photo courtesy of Cliff House

Above left: Dan Hountalas of Cliff House. Photo courtesy of Kimberley Lovato

Above right: Cliff House front. Photo courtesy of Cliff House

COOKIE LOVE

And they called it Cookie Love

Who doesn't have a memory of warm cookies in Grandma's kitchen? In the case of Cookie Love owner Erika Olson, it was her mother's kitchen where they baked together and then licked the mixer beaters clean of dough. The recollection has stayed with Erika throughout her life. Even after college, she says, she was serious about opening a cookie-dough company. But as happens with many young people, Erika was too uncertain and felt the pull of a "real" job.

For nearly two decades she traveled the world, working in product marketing for Continental Airlines and luxury brand Bulgari. While it fed her love of travel, it did little for her cookie dreams, which had all but crumbled. So she quit her high-powered job and moved to Barcelona for a year to fashion a new future. A job offer from another large luxury goods company was the impetus she needed to take the now-or-never cookie plunge. Having lived on and off in San Francisco when she wasn't on an airplane, Erika says she got to know other neighborhood cookie shops—Hot Cookie and Anthony's being her go-to favorites—and felt there was room for one more.

She found her sweet shop and painted it bright turquoise blue, and Cookie Love opened in 2015, on May 15, an auspicious date as it happens to be National Chocolate Chip Day. Erika and a small team make about three hundred cookies a day, including classics such

> "When cupcakes became the country's dessert obsession, I thought, 'Why not cookies?'"
> ~Erika Olson

Top right: The Cookie Love menu is full of favorites and unusual treats. Photo courtesy of Kimberley Lovato

Above left: Erika Olson shows off her sugar cookie love. Photo courtesy of Kimberley Lovato

Above right: The sign says it all. Photo courtesy of Kimberley Lovato

as snickerdoodle, sugar with rainbow sprinkles, and milk chocolate chip. But Erika's expertise shines with her unusual flavors, such as butterscotch banana, lavender white chocolate, and her personal favorite—milk chocolate blueberry. Her potato chip pecan satisfies lovers of salty-sweet treats, while the s'more tastes like camping, without the fuss of the tent or the fire.

1488 Pine St.
415-829-7449
www.cookielovesf.com
Neighborhood: Nob Hill

CRAB LOUIS

Loo-ey! Loo-ey!

No matter how you spell it—Louie or Louis—it is pronounced Loo-ey, and the salad is an old-fashioned character in the San Francisco culinary narrative, with an origin that is still up for debate. A mélange of lettuce, tomatoes, hard-boiled eggs, and lumps of fresh Dungeness crab, the salad has had a few costume changes over the years, and restaurants like to put their own accent on the original. Historians concur that it first appeared in West Coast eateries in the early 1900s, and two San Francisco establishments—Solari's Restaurant and the Westin St. Francis—claim it as their creation.

Another story credits a chef at Seattle's Olympic Club, and still another nods to the Davenport Hotel in Spokane, Washington, whose owner, Llewellyn "Louis" Davenport, arrived from San Francisco in 1889 and added it to the hotel restaurant's menu.

Try it.

Woodhouse Fish Co. serves crab in countless ways, including in a crisp Crab Louis salad.
1914 Fillmore St., 415-437-2722
www.woodhousefish.com

Swan Oyster Depot is a seafood institution serving Crab Louis, among other favorites.
1517 Polk St., 415-673-1101

Cliff House serves a version of the classic, adding citrus fruit, avocados, and cucumber.
1090 Point Lobos Ave., 415-386-3330
www.cliffhouse.com

Top: Crab Louis salad is old-school SF. Photo courtesy of Bea D'Amico

Bottom: The Crab Louis salad from Cliff House. Photo courtesy of Cliff House

DANDELION CHOCOLATE

Bean-to-bar by the Bay

It is a familiar entrepreneur story in Silicon Valley: create a start-up in your garage, basement, or cubicle, sell it to a bigger company for an obscene amount of money, and repeat. But the variable for Todd Masonis was a passion for chocolate. Instead of investing in another tech endeavor, he decided to put his money where his mouth was, literally. After Todd sold his company in 2008, he and his wife traveled to France, where they visited chocolatiers, chocolate shops, confectioners, and a family-run chocolate maker in Lyon, and he recalls being enamored of the thick and decadent chocolate drinks at Jean-Paul Hévin's salon and Angelina in Paris.

Todd's first foray into making chocolate was to do it at home in his kitchen. He and his friend, Cameron Ring, then decided to take over a friend's garage and make larger batches. "At that time you really had to build or repurpose your own machinery, which involved a lot of duct tape and trips to Home Depot," says Todd. What started as a curiosity-fueled hobby turned into awards and customers knocking on their door. That's when he and Cameron decided to go for it and build a small bean-to-bar factory and café in the Mission, which opened in 2013. Todd travels to meet his producers, who grow, ferment, and dry beans using best practices in places like Papua New Guinea, Belize, Madagascar, and Ecuador. Each varietal and origin has its own taste

> "It's important to make this distinction: A chocolatier buys chocolate and turns it into different candies. A chocolate maker sources and roasts good beans and turns them into chocolate."
> ~Todd Masonis

EVENTS & CLASSES

DATE	NAME	SPECIAL EVENTS
3/5, 3/8, 3/15, 3/19	Chocolate 101: an Introduction	Sourcing Talk: Maya Mountain
3/5, 3/12, 3/19, 3/26	Chocolate 201: hands-on	-Learn about the producers
2/23, 3/23	Sake and Chocolate	latest bar from Maya Mountain
	Parent/Child Chocolate 201	3/16 - 6:30pm
3/12, 4/9, 4/23	Children's Chocolate Exploration	
3/12, 4/9	Children's Chocolate Apprentice	From Code to Cacao
2/7, 3/7, 4/4	Visita guiada de la fabrica	-Greg D will share how he r
		3/20 - 7pm	UC Berkeley

Top left: Todd Masonis of Dandelion Chocolate. Photo courtesy of Molly DeCoudreaux

Top right: Beans are hand sorted. Photo courtesy of Kimberley Lovato

Above left: Each bar produced is individually wrapped with a label that tells the story of the bean. Photo courtesy of Kimberley Lovato

Above right: Chocolate education means tasty homework. Photo courtesy of Kimberley Lovato

and complexities, not unlike wine or coffee, Todd says. That's why Dandelion uses only two ingredients—cocoa beans and organic cane sugar—to let the true flavor of the bean and its origin shine. It's also why he put the entire factory on display, "so customers could see exactly what we are doing." One thing Todd says he's learned since starting Dandelion is that the Bay Area has a long history of chocolate makers, from Ghirardelli and Guittard to Scharffen Berger and TCHO. Dandelion is now another character in that sweet history.

740 Valencia St.
415-349-0942
www.dandelionchocolate.com
Neighborhood: Mission

67

DELI BOARD

A San Francisco deli-cacy

In search of East Coast and Midwest deli classics with a California twist? Look no further than this South of Market celebration of the mighty sandwich. It is run by Adam Mesnick, a self-proclaimed Deli Dude and proud Clevelander who left his hometown for a bread-and-butter career in mortgage banking and ended up rolling in a different kind of bread—sourdough, French, rye, Dutch Crunch. On it he piles lean pastrami, brisket, corned beef, turkey, kosher salami, roast beef, and daring combos of all to create his sandwiches, called "sandos" in Deli Board-ese.

Pay close attention to their names, which represent people Adam knows, or fond memories. LRB, for example, is a chicken salad sandwich named after his niece, who loves it. The Gold-n-Berg-n-Stein, stacked with corned beef, Romanian pastrami, kosher salami, cole slaw, Muenster cheese, and Thousand Island dressing, is a name Adam once considered for his deli, but it doesn't slip off the tongue (or type into search engines) quite as easily as Deli Board. Adam looks at his sandwiches the way Romeo looks at Juliet, and he says food has been a passion all his life. He spent a lot of time in his grandmother's kitchen watching her cook and worked as a short-order cook during college.

When the banking industry hit the skids, Adam followed his stomach to a commercial kitchen, where he started a catering

> "Many of the sandwich combos at Deli Board were in notebooks I kept in my early teens."
> ~Adam Mesnick

Left: Adam Mesnick. Photo courtesy of Rena B. Meyer

Right: Deli Board sandwiches are a hot lunchtime commodity. Photo courtesy of Rena B. Meyer

business, making soup, sandwiches, and homemade sauces. Tapping into San Francisco's fleet of bike messengers, Adam began selling door-to-door to the companies he'd once done business with. When customers started showing up at his kitchen window, he knew he had to find a place of his own.

Deli Board opened in 2012, coincidentally just around the corner from Cleveland Street—a sure sign that Adam has finally found his perfect role: the chairman of the Deli Board, with a loyal following of sando disciples who never seem to tire of his winning combos.

1058 Folsom St.
415-552-7687
www.deliboardsf.com
Neighborhood: SoMa

DOC RICKETTS

What's up (downstairs), Doc?

Until the fabled Purple Onion comedy club closed in 2012, it was as much of a fixture in San Francisco as the fog. For nearly sixty years, scores of comedians such as Bob Newhart, Richard Pryor, Robin Williams, Woody Allen, Lenny Bruce, and an East Bay housewife named Phyllis Diller brought laughs to the brick-walled basement.

When Christopher Burnett was looking for a space for a restaurant, he says it was hard to resist the derelict building and its history, which directed his vision. Two years of renovation later, he opened Doc Ricketts, an above-ground restaurant, and Doc's Lab, the downstairs enclave that continues the Purple Onion tradition of showcasing artists, musicians, and entertainers.

An added bonus is chef Kurt Steeber dishing out some of the best food at any live venue in the city, including housemade charcuterie, a ground short-rib burger, and a fried chicken dinner, all washed down with handcrafted cocktails and downstairs good times that are livin' it up anew.

Ed Ricketts was a California marine biologist who gathered writers, scientists, and artists in his "lab" during the '30s and '40s. He inspired the character of "Doc" in John Steinbeck's *Cannery Row* and the name of this restaurant and club.

Top: Great food and cocktails are always on stage. Photo courtesy of Gabriel Rojas

Above left: Doc's Lab carries on the live entertainment tradition of the Purple Onion. Photo courtesy of Gabriel Rojas

Above right: The upstairs dining room serves lunch and dinner. Photo courtesy of Gabriel Rojas

124 Columbus Ave.
415-649-6191
www.docrickettssf.com
Neighborhood: North Beach/Jackson Square

THE DOUGLAS ROOM

Bar food grows up

The Douglas Room hides a savory secret. At first glance it's a trendy drinking den favored by San Francisco's cocktail glitterati, but ask for a menu and you'll discover a killer brunch, lunch, dinner, and late-night snacking spot that nails grown-up bar food. There are the standby wings (of duck confit); a burger (made with Waygu beef); and there is Cheese Whiz. Yep, it's on the Whiz Wit sandwich, a ribeye and caramelized onion homage to the Philly cheesesteak. Even the Amoroso roll is flown in from Philadelphia. Masterminding The Douglas Room are Mo Hodges (a Philly native) and Brian Felley, the star bartenders behind San Francisco's beloved Benjamin Cooper, and chef Glen Schwartz, formerly at Campton Place. "I hate to say we elevate our bar food better than all others because the dining scene in San Francisco is outstanding. That being said, our chefs consistently amaze our customers with their imaginative specials and menu staples," says Brian. Imagination seems to be the common thread throughout the setting. The historic 1928 building, now the Tilden Hotel and home to The Douglas Room, is in the Tenderloin, a neighborhood that boomed in the Depression Era for working class and creative San Franciscans. Brian and Mo, along with hotel owner Stephen Yang, were drawn to the

Douglas Tilden was an internationally acclaimed California sculptor whose magnificent monuments, including *The Mechanics* at Bush, Battery, and Market Streets, still decorate the city.

Top left: Cocktails, art, and food meet at the Tilden Hotel. Photo courtesy of Kelly Puleio

Above right: Duck confit wings—not your average bar food. Photo courtesy of Kelly Puleio

Above left: The Whiz Wit is SF's answer to the Philly cheesesteak. Photo courtesy of Kelly Puleio

idea of the Tilden as a creative and community-friendly place with a commitment to neighborhood artists. Check out the four large-scale pieces in the lobby from local Jenny Kiker. Artist Joe Papagoda has been commissioned to create a massive mural, and there is even a poet-in-residence, Jessie Johnson, a Tenderloin wordsmith producing exclusive writing for the hotel. "The Tenderloin is a colorful cornucopia of different people, from the young affluence that's moving into the neighborhood to an impoverished artist community that's been here for generations," says Brian. "We are excited to be a part of its future."

345 Taylor St.
www.tildenhotel.com
415-673-2332
Neighborhood: Tenderloin

DUNGENESS CRAB

Cracked up

It's the most wonderful time of the year in San Francisco—crab season—when markets, restaurants, and holiday tables overflow with this favorite wintertime delicacy. Dungeness crab is found all along the Pacific Northwest coast. In fact, it gets its common (non-scientific) moniker from the town of Dungeness, in Washington State, but the spidery-looking, orange crustacean might as well be the mascot of San Francisco. Menus around the city brim with crabby creations, and piles of them are found fresh, cracked, and cleaned at stalls on Fisherman's Wharf. The season starts in November and officially runs until June, but most of the haul is brought in by the end of December, so get crackin' for a winter crab feast.

Try it.

Fisherman's Wharf is HQ for off-the-boat Dungeness crab.
www.visitfishermanswharf.com

Thanh Long boasts "world-famous roast crab since 1971," and
its crab with garlic noodles is legendary.
4101 Judah St.
415-665-1146
www.thanhlongsf.com

Swan Oyster Depot has long lines for many good reasons;
one of them is the crab.
1517 Polk St.
415-673-1101

Top right: Dungeness crab. Photo courtesy of San Francisco Travel Association

Above left: Eat it fresh from the source at Fisherman's Wharf. Photo courtesy of Kimberley Lovato

Above right: Crab stands on the wharf cook crab to order. Photo courtesy of Kimberley Lovato

THE EPICUREAN TRADER

An epicure's general store

There are many how-we-got-here stories floating around, but Holly McDell and her husband, Mat Pond, might have the best one yet.

It begins with drinks in Sydney, Australia, where, says Holly, the two of them decided to jot down names on a cocktail napkin of three cities they would like to live in. Mat wrote Paris, Buenos Aires, and San Francisco, while Holly chose New York, Brasilia, and San Francisco. A match! The next day they quit their jobs, and a few weeks later they landed on San Francisco's hilly doorstep, not knowing a single other person.

Holly and Mat both come from food families. They loved the idea of bringing high-quality gourmet products to San Francisco's sophisticated population of home cooks and food lovers, while supporting independent artisans from around the country. Holly and Mat spent six months researching, tasting, and reaching out to small-batch producers and are admittedly picky when it comes to their selections.

Holly laughs thinking about the spontaneity of it all. The one thing they knew, she says, was that San Francisco was the right place to give it a go because it is a city that loves food as much as supporting the little guy. Their Bernal Heights shop has an old-fashioned general store quality to it, staffed with food-passionate folks who embrace the answer-any-question ethos. Shelves are lined with a range of products, from well-known local brands such as Tartine bread and Humphry Slocombe ice cream to unheard-of makers of

The Epicurean Trader opened its second store on Union Street.

Top right: Products from small purveyors line the shelves. Photo courtesy of Kimberley Lovato

Above left: Holly McDell and Mat Pond. Photo courtesy of Kimberley Lovato

Above right: The original Bernal Heights shop opened in 2015. Photo courtesy of The Epicurean Trader

mustard, pickles, snacks, cotton candy, cheese, chocolate, honey, olive oil, and much in between.

Mat has also started a craft spirits and whiskey club, bringing his vetted monthly selections to members. They'd eventually like to host classes, but for now, says Holly, they are busy brand ambassadors for these small food purveyors, introducing them to a city the couple now happily calls home, at least until their next game of cocktail napkin roulette.

401 Courtland Ave.
415-872-9484
www.theepicureantrader.com
Neighborhood: Bernal Heights

FERRY BUILDING

San Francisco's most famous food hall

Before the Golden Gate and Bay Bridges were built in the 1930s, boats were the only way for commuters from across the bay to arrive in the city, and the Ferry Building was the point of entry. At one time, it was the second busiest transit terminal in the world (London's Charing Cross Station had it beat). Today, it's a downtown landmark, with a 245-foot clock tower modeled after the bell tower in Spain's Seville Cathedral. It is still a hub for waterborne transport, but the 119-year-old building is also a gourmet gauntlet of local food.

Pick up a crunchy loaf of Acme bread and top it with Boccalone salami, creamy or crumbly cheese from Cowgirl Creamery, and olive oil from McEvoy Ranch. Tomales Bay oysters from Hog Island Oyster Company are shucked before your eyes, and the flaky, handmade empanadas at El Porteño are made from the recipe of the owner's grandmother. Advanced reservations are a must at chef Charles Phan's nationally acclaimed Vietnamese restaurant, The Slanted Door. Brunch doesn't get better than at Boulettes Larder. For special occasions, or just because, the gorgeous cakes at Miette are worth celebrating, as is the golden sweet honey at Beekind.

1 Ferry Building
415-983-8030
www.ferrybuildingmarketplace.com
Neighborhood: Embarcadero

A popular farmers market is held here on
Saturdays, Tuesdays, and Thursdays.

Left: The Ferry Building hosts a weekly market. Photo courtesy of San Francisco Travel Association

Right: Inside the Ferry Building are numerous food shops and restaurants. Photo courtesy of Scott Chernis Photography

In addition to the Ferry Building's weekly market, several others roll out the best of the Golden State:

Alemany
Saturdays, 100 Alemany Blvd.

Mission Community Market
Thursdays, Bartlett St. at 22nd St.

Heart of the City
Sundays and Wednesdays, United Nations Plaza

Richmond
Sundays, Clement St., between 2nd and 4th Aves.

Fillmore
Saturdays, 1700 O'Farrell St.

FIOR D'ITALIA

The flower of San Francisco

When Fior d'Italia opened on Broadway in 1886, the Gold Rush was in full swing, and San Francisco's tawdry soul lured miners, sailors, gamblers, and dreamers to its saloons, bordellos, and taverns. Angelo Del Monte came to America from Italy in search of gold, too. Unsuccessful, he settled in San Francisco, striking gold in another way—by serving food to the city's hungry fortune seekers. Immigrant Armido "Papa" Marianetti later joined him, and the duo laid the groundwork that would turn the Fior d'Italia, the "flower of Italy," into what is now the oldest Italian restaurant in the United States.

The original building on Broadway burned down, as did the next following the 1906 earthquake. After address hopping around North Beach and changing owners a few times, too, Fior d'Italia, often called the Fior, took root on the corner of Stockton and Union Streets, where it stayed for more than fifty years. A Valentine's Day fire in 2005 forced the Fior to move yet again, this time to the charming San Remo Hotel, its sixth North Beach location.

For a moment in 2012, current owners chef Gianni Audieri and his wife, Trudy, only the fourth owners in the restaurant's history, thought the Fior would close for good when the previous proprietors decided to call it quits. Chef Audieri, who'd been in the kitchen for around thirty years, could not bear to let that happen, and he

> The building that is now the San Remo Hotel was built by Bank of America founder A. P. Giannini.

Top left: Chef Gianni and Trudy Audieri are only the fourth owners in Fior d'Italia's long history. Photo courtesy of Kimberley Lovato

Top right: Fior d'Italia, circa 1920s. Photo courtesy of Hotel San Remo

Above left: The Fior is a hub of Italian social life in San Francisco. Photo courtesy of Kimberley Lovato

Above right: The hotel that is now the San Remo was built by Bank of America founder A. P. Giannini. Photo courtesy of Kimberley Lovato

and Trudy managed to take it over, saving a slice of San Francisco history. Prior to arriving at the Fior, Gianni globe-trotted, serving his Northern Italian cuisine in his hometown of Milan; in New York, Switzerland, and London; on cruise ships; and in private clubs. He says when he arrived in San Francisco, it reminded him of Italy. He was home. Decades of San Francisco Italians have considered the Fior their cultural and social home, too. We can only hope the flower of Italy blooms for new generations, and for another 130 years.

2237 Mason St.
415-986-1886
www.fior.com
Neighborhood: North Beach

FORBES ISLAND

One man's home

If a man's home is his castle, then what do you call a manmade island built from barges, complete with palm trees, a lighthouse, and a sandy beach? In San Francisco the answer is Forbes Island, a kitschy, bizarre, and one-of-a-kind restaurant floating off Pier 39. But before the one-hundred-foot-long, seven-hundred-ton oddity fed curious out-of-towners, Forbes Island was the obsession of its creator, Forbes Thor Kiddoo, a floating-home builder in Sausalito during the 1970s.

According to his longtime friend Erick Hendricks, who has been the restaurant's general manager since it opened in 1999, Forbes is an eccentric (no kidding!) and came up with a kooky idea: instead of just building floating homes, why not build a little piece of real estate? He named his slice Forbes Island and anchored it off the shores of Sausalito. The nautical curio had three staterooms, a large salon, a fireplace, a wine cellar, and even a grand piano on board. It attracted attention from media, too, making appearances on '80s reality TV shows *That's Incredible!* and *Lifestyles of the Rich and Famous*. But complaints from Sausalito residents and battles with the city chased Forbes Island to the welcoming waters off San Francisco, where it was converted into a restaurant.

Reservation holders hop aboard the ferry at Pier 39 for a four-minute jaunt to the idiosyncratic isle, where they can climb to the top of the lighthouse for a pre-dinner view of the San Francisco skyline, Alcatraz, and the Golden Gate Bridge. A prix fixe, four-course meal

About four hundred people per week visit Forbes Island.

Top: So close to Pier 39 you can hear the seals bark. Photo courtesy of Kimberley Lovato

Above left: The island was once the home of a local barge builder. Photo courtesy of Forbes Island

Above right: The downstairs dining room. Photo courtesy of Forbes Island

is served downstairs in a one-hundred-seat dining room, and Forbes's former red velvet bedroom is now part of the ladies lounge. Erick says his eighty-year-old friend is not around as much as he used to be but still pops in from time to time to wax nostalgic about his creation, which easily ranks as one of San Francisco's quirkiest places to dine out.

415-951-4900
www.forbesisland.com
Neighborhood: Fisherman's Wharf

FOREIGN CINEMA

Date night done right

For a different twist on dinner and a movie, Foreign Cinema gets top billing. The acclaimed restaurant in the Mission District is popular for Sunday brunch oysters and champagne, but it's the classic movies flickering on the patio's back wall that up the ante for date night. The films are an attraction, for sure, but Foreign Cinema isn't consistently ranked as one of the city's best restaurants because of its good looks. Chef Gayle Pirie, who, with her partner, chef John Clark, took over the space a little more than a year after it opened in 1999, dazzles diners with seasonal and stylish California cuisine in a neighborhood where new hotspots frequently fizzle out.

Gayle recalls the early days when she and John were trailblazers, working to build the restaurant's reputation—and their own—in a neighborhood that was known more for dodgy surroundings than as a dining destination. The transformation over the past ten years is nothing short of mind-boggling. Just ask any San Franciscan trying to book a table or rent an apartment in the neighborhood today. Gayle likes to say that entering Foreign Cinema is like falling through a rabbit hole. Pull open the geometric entry doors on gritty Mission Street, walk down a darkened corridor, and arrive in a light-filled industrial space facing a romantic courtyard strung with Edison lights. It delivers a sensual experience before you even crack open the menu.

> "We always wanted this to be a beloved institution, accessible to everyone."
> ~Gayle Pirie

Top left: Chef/owners John Clark and Gayle Pirie have turned Foreign Cinema into a San Francisco mainstay. Photo courtesy of Charlie Villyard

Top right: The outdoor courtyard is the place to dine at Foreign Cinema. Photo courtesy of Charlie Villyard

Above left: Entry to Foreign Cinema. Photo courtesy of Kimberley Lovato

Above right: Sunday brunch isn't just a meal, it's an event at Foreign Cinema. Photo courtesy of Charlie Villyard

Contrary to local lore, Foreign Cinema was not once a movie theater. However, it does pay homage to the heyday of independent movie houses that speckled San Francisco in the 1940s, when five independent theaters lined six blocks of Mission Street. In a city whose restaurant landscape shifts like rolling fog, celebrity is hard to pull off, but there's no doubt Foreign Cinema is destined for San Francisco's hall of fame.

2534 Mission St.
415-648-7600
www.foreigncinema.com
Neighborhood: Mission

FORTUNE COOKIES

Chronicles of a cookie

Although we enjoy them after every Chinese meal, the sweet fortune cookie as we know it is really an American invention, believed to have started right here in San Francisco. Its origin, however, is in Japan, where bakers outside Shinto shrines hand folded savory crackers, like *senbei*, and placed "o-mikuji," a fortune written on a slip of paper, inside. So how did the vanilla-infused cookies with messages of health, love, and winning lottery numbers arrive in San Francisco? A widely accepted story is that Makoto Hagiwara, a Japanese gardener who tended to Japanese Tea Garden in San Francisco's Golden Gate Park, introduced them around the turn of the century and served them with tea to garden visitors. He's said to have sweetened the recipe for local taste, and a Japantown bakery called Benkyodo supplied the garden until Japanese-American internment during World War II. It is believed that Chinese-American businessmen seized the opportunity to produce the cookies and sold them to Chinese restaurants.

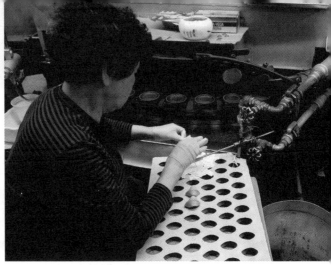

Left: A tranquil scene at the Japanese Tea Garden in Golden Gate Park. Photo courtesy of San Francisco Travel Association

Right: Fortune cookies in Chinatown. Photo courtesy of Kimberley Lovato

Try it.
The Golden Gate Fortune Cookie Factory has been making
them in Chinatown since 1962.
56 Ross Alley
415-781-3956

Mee Mee Bakery makes vanilla as well as chocolate,
strawberry, and supersized cookies.
1328 Stockton St.
415-362-3204
www.meemeebakery.com/visitus

FRENA BAKERY

Israeli delights

Name a part of the planet whose food you'd like to eat, and you will stumble over the opportunity to try it somewhere in San Francisco—or so thought the trio behind Frena, San Francisco's only kosher bakery. Owners Isaac Yosef, Avi Edri, and fourth-generation baker Yanni, who prefers his one-name moniker (like Prince or Sting), hail from Israel but met at a Hanukkah party in San Francisco, where they reminisced about the food they'd grown up with and the lack of it in their adopted hometown.

Isaac recalls dashing into many a bakery and leaving empty handed and disappointed, not because the bakeries were bad but because there was so much sweet food. He craved good pita bread and *sambusak*, savory turnover pastries commonly found in Jerusalem and Tel Aviv. One night Yanni baked pita at his house, and Isaac recalls that the taste was like home.

The friends hatched a business plan to fill the void. When they opened in December 2016, the response was overwhelming. Yanni uses recipes from his great-grandfather, who was a baker in Jerusalem's renowned Machane Yehuda market. Isaac says he's even seen a few people with tears in their eyes after tasting familiar but long-forgotten flavors. While they aim to serve those who keep kosher, the trio also hopes curiosity attracts anyone eager to discover new food and a different culture. Isaac and Avi are often found answering questions and handing out samples, and their

The name Frena comes from an ancient Moroccan oven and type of fluffy bread.

Top left: Kosher baked goods are made fresh daily. Photo courtesy of Frena

Top right: Specialties of Israel are baked daily. Photo courtesy of Frena

Above left: Sufganiyah, a traditional Hanukkah jelly doughnut, is made every day. Photo courtesy of Frena

Above right: The oven is where all the bakery magic happens. Photo courtesy of Frena

pita bread is nothing like the store-bought variety you think you love. Fresh challah, authentic bagels, and burekas—puff pastries of spinach, cheese, or potato—are also best sellers, along with the sufganiyah, a jelly-filled doughnut typically eaten during Hanukkah but made every day at Frena. Watching a kid bite into the treat as the powdered sugar dusts his eyelashes is one of the many joys seen at Frena, says Isaac, as is knowing he and his friends are bringing the taste of their childhood to a new generation half a world away.

132 Sixth St.
628-444-3666
www.frenabakery.com
Neighborhood: SoMa

GHIRARDELLI SQUARE

Domingo and the chocolate factory

When Domingo Ghirardelli immigrated to the United States in 1849, he, like many, planned to strike it rich in the California Gold Rush. But after panning and mining for the elusive precious metal to no avail, he found another line of work. He opened a store in Stockton, California, selling supplies and some confections to other miners, that was successful enough to allow him to move to San Francisco.

After a few years of trial and error, including opening the Cairo Coffee House, Domingo ultimately founded a confectionery company called Ghirardely & Gerard, which would lay the foundation for today's Ghirardelli Chocolate Company.

In need of larger manufacturing space in 1893, the Ghirardelli family moved the company to the Pioneer Woolen Mill building on the northern waterfront, where present-day Ghirardelli Square is found. Over the following years, an apartment building was built for employees and a power plant was added, along with a clock tower—still standing at the corner of Larkin and North Point Streets—designed after the Chateau de Blois in France. Two floors were added to a warehouse in 1923, and atop that those famous fifteen-foot-high letters spelling "Ghirardelli" that can be seen for miles. The company continues to flourish but is no longer run by the Ghirardelli family.

Ghirardelli Square hosts an annual Chocolate Festival each September, with 100 percent of the profits donated to Project Open Hand.

Left: Ghirardelli Square is an entertainment destinaton on the waterfront. Photo courtesy of Ghirardelli Square

Right: Historic truck. Photo courtesy of Ghirardelli Square

Golden Grain Macaroni Company, which was later acquired by Quaker Oats, bought it in 1963. Today, Lindt and Sprüngli is the parent company of Ghirardelli. Chocolate manufacturing has moved from San Francisco to the East Bay, but there are still plenty of reasons to visit this San Francisco historic site. The mixed-use space has a hotel, casual and upscale restaurants, art galleries, shops, a wine tasting room, and of course Ghirardelli ice cream and chocolate shops. Ghirardelli is the country's longest continuously operating chocolate manufacturer, and some of the old buildings where the company grew up are listed on the National Register of Historic Places, officially etching Domingo Ghirardelli's dream into American history. Eureka! It turns out he struck gold after all.

900 N. Point St.
415-474-3938
www.ghirardellisq.com
Neighborhood: Fisherman's Wharf

GREENS

Vegetarian visionary

Long gone are the days when vegetarian cuisine meant lifeless salads or bland meat substitutes, and we have Greens to thank for the enlightenment. The restaurant was founded by the San Francisco Zen Center in 1979 with a kitchen run by chef Deborah Madison, who revolutionized vegetarian cuisine, moving it from sustenance to sensational. Chef Annie Somerville took over in 1985 and has elevated vegetarian cuisine to its gourmet and mainstream status.

She refers to Greens as groundbreaking in its day, with imaginative and flavorful dishes made with fresh farm and dairy ingredients long before it was trendy to do so, and served by Zen students and monks.

The mission of Greens has not changed, and Annie's goal remains to serve outstanding food to the public, employ a large staff, and support a large web of farmers, producers, cheesemakers, and winemakers who use best environmental practices. Annie has also published two cookbooks, *Fields of Greens* and *Everyday Greens,* that bring gorgeous Greens recipes to home cooks around the world. Where vegetarian cooking was once considered an alternative lifestyle, Deborah, Annie, and Greens changed mindsets by showcasing just how tasty and sophisticated plant-based cooking can be. Judging from the crowds that pack into the 130-seat restaurant, it appears Greens is adored by gastronomes who appreciate the seasonal, flavor-packed menu of dishes such as fire-roasted poblano chili with goat cheese, avocado,

> "We feel very fortunate to be in this extraordinary city, right on the edge of San Francisco Bay."
> ~Annie Somerville

Top left: Chef Annie Somerville took vegetarian cuisine mainstream. Photo courtesy of Annie Somerville

Top right: A meal at Greens is as satisfying as it is healthy. Photo courtesy of Kimberley Lovato

Above: Fort Mason in San Francisco's Marina District. Photo courtesy of Kimberley Lovato

and crème fraîche and roasted figs and burrata that flow from the creative kitchen. The dining room is also a destination, spread out in a restored Army warehouse with floor-to-ceiling windows that look onto a marina, the bay, and the Golden Gate Bridge. More than three decades since blazing a trail that changed the way we think of vegetarian, Greens is still doing what it does best: inspiring us to think differently.

Golden Gate Recreation Area, Landmark Building A
Fort Mason Center, 2 Marina Blvd.
415-771-6222
www.greensrestaurant.com
Neighborhood: Marina

THE GROVE

San Francisco's living room

There is nothing pretentious about The Grove, which is why it's been a San Francisco favorite for more than twenty years. It's the cozy café where friends kick off their weekend over coffee, where first dates spark or fizzle, and where owner Ken Zankel says parents can feel at ease letting their kids drop Cheerios all over the floor while they drink a bottle of wine.

Since the first location opened in 1996, The Grove has blossomed in three other locations around San Francisco, with a fourth on the way. But don't for a second think of this as a cookie-cutter chain. Ken and his wife, Anna, have ensured that each location renders a unique soulfulness via design touches that tie into the duo's love of music, travel, and family. In their Fillmore location you'll see Ken's old electric guitar, which he played during his brother's wedding. At the Hayes Valley outpost, American and California flags that once flew over Anna's family home are framed on the wall. Even The Grove's logo features their dog with Ken's Gretsch guitar in its mouth, in a grove of trees like the one Anna grew up in. The two met when Ken, a native New Yorker, moved to San Francisco and decided to open a pizza place (to show Californians how it's done). He hired Anna as his interior designer. A few collaborations later, including The Grove's original Chestnut Street location (now closed), and Ken finally summoned the nerve to ask Anna out.

> "For us The Grove has always been a personal endeavor."
> ~Ken Zankel

Top right: Personal touches, such as lion heads (Anna and Ken are Leos), highlight each location. Photo courtesy of Lori Eanes

Above left: Anna, Ken, and their dog, Baron. Photo courtesy of Lori Eanes

Above right: The Grove on Fillmore Street is a Pacific Heights favorite. Photo courtesy of Lori Eanes

They liken The Grove's locations to siblings because each has a similar personality and look, with stone fireplaces, barn-wood floors, and a to-die-for soundtrack. The uncontrived authenticity is found on the menu too, with familiar meals such as mac and cheese, fresh salads, homemade enchiladas, and chicken pot pie. They say they have always liked restaurants that embody their owners, and they tried to mimic that feel at The Grove. It works, as if you've been invited into Ken and Anna's living room to kick up your feet, unwind, and make yourself at home.

2016 Fillmore St.
415-474-1419
www.thegrovesf.com
Neighborhood: Pacific Heights

HANG AH TEA ROOM

A little touch of heart

San Francisco's Chinatown is full of surprises, and Hang Ah Tea Room might be the littlest one you've never heard of. The hard-to-find restaurant is removed from the paper lanterns and tourist shops of Grant Street, yet it sports a title that might attract many: the oldest dim sum restaurant in the United States. It's a fact that surprised owner Frank Chui. As a child, he played basketball and volleyball on the cement playground across the alleyway, and he recalls that the restaurant was perpetually closed.

In 2013, while Frank was working in the telecom industry, his friend alerted him to a small Chinatown dim sum restaurant on Pagoda Place that was for sale. It rang a bell. Hang Ah Tea Room had opened in 1920 and served Chinatown's growing immigrant population. Frank says the more he dug into the history, the more he was drawn to the idea of keeping alive this Chinatown legacy. With nearly one hundred years of history under its belt, the restaurant has changed hands many times, and when Frank and his business partner, Billy Lai, bought it, they met the elderly couple who had been running it.

Frank says they rarely opened Hang Ah in the end and didn't really care about the place, but didn't want to see Hang Ah's history die out either. The couple stuck around for a few months to help Frank and Billy learn the recipes for specialties such as hai gow (shrimp dumplings), gin cha siu bao (barbecue pork buns), chung yao ban (scallion pancakes), and xiao long bao (soup dumplings), along with other dim sum—two words that Frank says translate to "touch of

Hang Ah Tea Room has a website now for takeout orders.

Top: Hang Ah Tea Room doesn't look like much from outside, but don't be fooled. Photo courtesy of Basil Vargas

Above left: Dim sum translates to "a touch of heart" in Chinese. Photo courtesy of Basil Vargas

Above right: Frank Chui chills out. Photo courtesy of Basil Vargas

heart" in Chinese. Frank did away with what he calls the "Chinatown hours" and put signs out on bigger streets to lure pedestrians down Pagoda Alley. "Every day people call to see if we are really open or wander in for the first time," says Frank. "It's a new discovery of an old place."

1 Pagoda Place, 415-982-5686

www.hangah1920.com

Neighborhood: Chinatown

HANGTOWN FRY

Gold Rush grub

Though it's basically a breaded oyster and bacon omelet (sometimes with added scallions and tomatoes), the one-skillet meal tastes better seasoned with Gold Rush Era lore and a name born in the foothill mining town of Placerville, once known as "Hangtown" thanks to prolific hangings that occurred there. Rumor has it a prospector who'd struck it rich in the nearby creek pushed through the saloon doors of the El Dorado Hotel, where the Cary House Hotel now stands, and demanded the most expensive items on the menu, which were eggs, oysters, and bacon. Others say it was a condemned man who ordered the provisions. Either way, the cook scrambled 'em up and a dish was born. Like the miners and their riches, Hangtown fry also found its way to San Francisco. Though the recipe has likely morphed over the years, the rare menu find is an edible link to the Old West and worth its weight in historical gold.

Try it.
Tadich Grill has been serving Hangtown fry for 168 years.
240 California St.
415-391-1849
www.tadichgrill.com

Brenda's French Soul Food serves it with a side of grits and a biscuit
for a Southern twist.
652 Polk St.
415-345-8100
www.frenchsoulfood.com

Hangtown fry has been on Tadich Grill's menu since 1849. Photo courtesy of Jay Singh

Sam's Grill & Seafood Restaurant serves Hangtown fry and a slew of other historic favorites, indoors and out.
374 Bush St.
415-421-0594
www.samsgrillsf.com

HUMPHRY SLOCOMBE

Expect the unexpected

With a name like Humphry Slocombe, one might expect the proprietor to be a lovable "uncle" type in a knitted cardigan and sensible shoes. But the men behind the moniker at this small ice cream shop are called Sean Vahey and Jake Godby, and they resemble no such person. Jake, a shy former pastry chef of some of the city's best restaurants, and Sean, a stylish and hospitable veteran of posh hotels, are Humphry Slocombe. So where does the fuddy-duddy name come from? A 1970s British comedy series the duo loved called *Are You Being Served?* whose main characters were Mr. Humphries and Mrs. Slocombe. In San Francisco the name is synonymous with curious flavors that sport out-of-the-ordinary names and ingredients not often found in ice cream or sorbet.

The challenge will be choosing between the likes of Blueberry Boy Bait, I Have a Dreamsicle, Elvis: The Fat Years, and dozens of others that Jake conjures up in his kitchen-laboratory. By far the best seller, and the flavor that launched a thousand Humphry Slocombe devotees, is Secret Breakfast, a combo of Jake's homemade extra-crispy cornflake cookies and bourbon—ice cream for grownups, say Sean and Jake. "Humphry Slocombe is old-fashioned in the sense that it handmakes every bit of ice cream, but it has modern sensibility," says Sean.

The *Humphry Slocombe Ice Cream Book* highlights forty recipes that bring its deliciousness home.

Left: A scoop of Blueberry Boy Bait. Photo courtesy of Humphry Slocombe

Right: Founders Sean Vahey and Jake Godby. Photo courtesy of Humphry Slocombe

When asked why the "unusual" flavors, Jake's answer comes quickly. "I do not think of them as unusual at all because that implies there are rules to be followed." Jake's do-your-own-thing mantra works well in a city that embraces outliers with open arms and palates and that has been known to break a rule or two.

2790 A Harrison St.
415-550-6971
www.humphryslocombe.com
Neighborhood: Mission

A gustatory gallery

If imitation is the sincerest form of flattery, then chefs around the world must be blushing, big time. The San Francisco Museum of Modern Art (SFMOMA) was one of the city's most anticipated reopenings of 2016, after a three-year closure and renovation that resulted in more gallery space and an eye-catching new building behind the already rather striking one. A new signature restaurant was also added. Called In Situ, the restaurant presents beautifully plated dishes culled from the recipes of famous chefs around the world.

Overseen by acclaimed chef Corey Lee (three-star Michelin chef of Benu), In Situ offers something that complements a visitor experience at SFMOMA. Corey says it was logical that the menu he created should feature many different chefs, not just one, which he rotates on and off the menu like oeuvres in a gallery. To accomplish this, Corey emailed chefs around the world, from Alice Waters of Chez Panisse in Berkeley to Pascal Barbot of Astrance in Paris, France, to Hiroshi Sasaki of Gion Sasaki in Kyoto, Japan, and invited them to participate. Around sixty-five agreed. They were free to select the recipe as well as how they wanted to teach it to Corey's team. Some preferred to send very detailed instructions, Corey says, while others sent video tutorials, emails, or photos of various stages of the recipes. Corey also visited chefs that preferred to teach the dish in person, while other chefs came to In Situ. The result is a

"We hope that all guests will feel a sense of discovery by trying something from a chef or restaurant that they may have never heard of or had the opportunity to experience."
~Chef Corey Lee

Top: In Situ is a gallery within a museum, with artistic dishes from chefs around the globe. Photo courtesy of Eric Wolfinger

Above left: Chef Corey Lee's restaurant In Situ sits on the ground floor of the San Francisco Museum of Modern Art. Photo courtesy of Eric Wolfinger

Above right: Corey Lee's interpretaton of a dish from Mirazur in Menton, France. Photo courtesy of Eric Wolfinger

new edible exhibition every four to six weeks showcasing the work of renowned artists who happen to be some of the world's most innovative chefs.

Whether it's the wasabi lobster from Tim Raue of Restaurant Tim Raue in Berlin, Germany; the Forest from Mauro Colagreco of Mirazur in Menton, France; or a lettuce wrap from Anthony Myint of Mission Street Food in San Francisco, at In Situ, life imitates art in the most delicious way.

In Situ at SFMOMA, 151 Third St., 415-941-6050
www.insitu.sfmoma.org, Neighborhood: SoMa

JOHN'S GRILL

Literary chops

Though this downtown restaurant has been around since 1908, the literati have made it a pilgrimage stop since author Dashiell Hammett penned his 1930 novel, *The Maltese Falcon*, in which gumshoe Sam Spade scours San Francisco for a jewel-encrusted statuette. Sam eats chops, a baked potato, and sliced tomatoes at John's Grill. Hammett worked nearby in the Flood Building in the 1920s and lived in an apartment on Post Street while writing the famous book, and fans of the famous falcon flock (bird pun intended) to John's Grill to snap photos and dine on standard steakhouse fare.

But there's a real live caper that Sam Spade didn't know about. Taking advantage of the restaurant's *Maltese Falcon* pedigree, the owners of John's Grill attempted to procure one of the original props used in the movie version of the book when it came up for auction in 1994. They failed to nab it, but they invited the statuette to a party at John's Grill, along with Hammett's family and one of the last surviving actors from the film.

Don Herron has led a Dashiell Hammett tour in San Francisco since 1977, making it the longest-running literary tour in the country.

Left: The historic restaurant is a favorite haunt for book lovers. Photo courtesy of Kimberley Lovato

Center: Steak, seafood, and literary intrigue are served. Photo courtesy of Kimberley Lovato

Right: A replica of the Maltese falcon perches behind glass. Photo courtesy of Kimberley Lovato

In lieu of the original prop, the owners purchased a plaster cast and asked the Hammett family and the actor to sign it before caging it in a glass cabinet for all eternity. Or so they thought. In 2007 the statue was stolen and has been missing ever since. The new lead and bronze bird perching in its place weighs 150 pounds and is much harder to stuff in your handbag. But you can dine on chops and a baked potato, listen to some live jazz, and let your imagination flutter around the local mystery. There are not many places in San Francisco serving this combo, but John's Grill delivers in Sam Spades.

63 Ellis St.
415-986-3274
www.johnsgrill.com
Neighborhood: Union Square

JOSEY BAKER BREAD

What's in a name?

When your last name is Baker, it's easy to presume the universe had a plan. But according to Josey Baker (yes, his real name), his flour-lined path was more of an accidental obsession than a planned profession. He'd moved from Vermont to San Francisco in 2005 to teach science.

Five years later, a friend gave him a fermenting lump of bread starter. With no background in cooking, Josey says he started playing around with it in his kitchen, baking trial-and-error style. It was love at first dough rise, and he says he found himself doing it all the time, baking loaves so often he gave them away to friends and sold them to neighbors.

One morning, he recalls, sixty strangers showed up at his door to buy bread. In 2011, San Francisco's popular Four Barrel Coffee approached him to collaborate on The Mill, a new café that opened in 2012 around the corner from the painted ladies of Alamo Square. Business has been booming since, but he still finds time to bake. Luckily a talented team of bakers helps him keep up with the demand of nearly four hundred loaves a day made with sustainably grown, organic ingredients and freshly milled whole-grain flour. Yes, there is actually a mill at The Mill. The names of each style of bread reflect Josey's happy-go-lucky style: Adventure Bread; Red, White + Rye; Purple Beauty; and Wonder Bread (not at all related to the spongy squares from polka-dotted bags of our childhood).

> "The success still doesn't feel real, but apparently it is."
> ~Josey Baker

Top left: Josey Baker. Photo courtesy of the Morrisons

Top right: The Mill is home to Josey Baker Bread. Photo courtesy of Kimberley Lovato

Above left: The Mill is where the magic happens. Photo courtesy of Kimberley Lovato

Above right: Josey Baker smiles. Photo courtesy of the Morrisons

In his spare time, Josey also managed to pen a cookbook, *Josey Baker Bread*, imploring novice kneaders to give it a go at home. His ever-present smile is as addictive as his bread, and what Josey says he loved about baking when he started out is still what drives him today. "Baking is a blend of scientific methodology and know-how with expressive creativity," he says. It turns out Josey was born a Baker and was destined to become one after all in San Francisco. Thank you, universe.

736 Divisadero St.
415-345-1953
www.joseybakerbread.com
Neighborhood: Alamo Square

LA FOLIE

A crazy idea

In French, La Folie can mean craziness, madness, or zaniness, and chef Roland Passot's petite restaurant started with a little bit of them all. He and his wife, Jamie, opened La Folie in 1988 with their talent and a little savings, but no name. Jamie suggested La Folie, she told Roland, because she thought they must be crazy to open a restaurant in finicky San Francisco with no money. The neighborhood, though abuzz today, was also a risk—so dead Roland says he could have played cards in the middle of the street and no one would have noticed.

For years, Roland and Jamie ate at La Folie and lived in a small apartment around the corner to be close to work. Thirty years on, the crazy, mad, zany idea appears to have paid off, for Roland and Jamie and for San Francisco. La Folie continues to rank as one of the nation's top restaurants, and Roland's roll call of awards and recognitions is as long as his wine list. In 2014, La Folie was chosen as the lunch spot for visiting French president François Hollande and several titans of the tech industry. A young Emmanuel Macron, elected president of France in 2017, was also present. Though La Folie doesn't normally serve lunch, Roland laughs, "When someone tells you the president of France is coming, you make it happen." Non-presidential types come, too, for the creative contemporary French cuisine exquisitely presented. But they return again and again for a different reason.

La Folie earned a Michelin star in 2015.

Top right: Contemporary French cuisine earned La Folie a Michelin star in 2015. Photo courtesy of La Folie

Above left: Chef Roland Passot is one of San Francisco's most acclaimed chefs. Photo courtesy of La Folie

Above right: Gorgeous food, artfully displayed. Photo courtesy of La Folie

La Folie's humble beginnings still guide the spirit of the elegant bistro. Even with all its glory and recognition, La Folie remains a family-run place, where Roland gets in the kitchen every day to work with his team and pops out to greet guests. "Many have been coming for generations and are as much a part of our family as we are theirs," says Roland. That's the kind of crazy we could all use a second helping of.

2316 Polk St.
415-776-5577
www.lafolie.com
Neighborhood: Polk Gulch/Russian Hill

LAZY BEAR

A super supper club

To call Lazy Bear a restaurant is an injustice. It's more of a cocktail party, wrapped in a unique experience, tied up with tasty supper club string.

Chef David Barzelay choreographs the convivial evening that combines the best of a dinner party vibe with San Francisco's dynamic dining scene. You'll start with appetizers in an upstairs living room, small talking and chatting with fellow guests, before David invites you to pull up a chair at two long tables in front of his wide-open kitchen for a multicourse meal punctuated by entertaining and engaging conversations. There's even a blank spot in the menu to note the names and contact info of your dining companions. It's the antithesis of the dining experiences David had. "When I ate out at nice restaurants I wanted to gush about the food and talk to people and see how things were made. Most places don't let you do that," he says.

David is not a trained chef. He is a trained lawyer. But that didn't stop him from reading food blogs and cookbooks, ordering cooking equipment, and daydreaming about menus during law school. When he took an internship in Austin, Texas, one year, he says he could suddenly afford to eat at better restaurants, and his interest in good food was piqued even more. Back at school, he realized the only way he'd be able to afford to eat like that regularly was if he learned to cook himself, so he did. David was laid off from his job as a lawyer in Silicon Valley in 2009, and he began hosting dinner parties at his

The name Lazy Bear is an anagram of Barzelay.

Top right: Chef David Barzelay greets guests. Photo courtesy of Kassie Borreson

Above left: It's not a restaurant, it's a dinner party. Photo courtesy of Kassie Borreson

Above right: The ultimate dinner party is at Lazy Bear. Photo courtesy of Kassie Borreson

apartment as well as staging at local restaurants, where he discovered he loved being in the kitchen. David's apartment parties became so popular that he found a larger space to hold his clandestine (and ironically not legal) dinners.

Five years later, Lazy Bear opened with its own name and address, 100 percent aboveboard. Each dinner party is a ticketed, pay-in-advance show that sells out within hours of being announced via social media or his newsletter. There are no plans to go back to law at this time. "I am having way too much fun," David says.

3416 Nineteenth St.
415-874-9921
www.lazybearsf.com
Neighborhood: Mission

LIGURIA BAKERY

Simple pleasures

There are not many, if any, places in the country where you'll find a focaccia bakery on the corner. But it's San Francisco, and we are lucky that way.

Liguria Bakery has been making the soft, flat Italian bread since Ambrogio Soracco brought his recipe from Genoa, Italy, in 1911. Now his grandson Michael continues the tradition. Peer through the glass at the empty shelves, and you might think the place is deserted. But stop by early in the morning and you'll see what all the fuss is about.

The bread is baked early each day in a brick oven and comes in several different varieties. The pizza version is popular, topped with tomato sauce and green onions. Liguria also sells olive, rosemary, and a raisin variety. The focaccia is sold in eight-inch by ten-inch rectangles, wrapped in white butcher paper, and tied up with string. It will definitely be one of your favorite things.

1700 Stockton St.
415-421-3786
Neighborhood: North Beach

Arrive early. When the focaccia is gone, the lights are dimmed, the door is locked, and Liguria closes up shop.

Top left: Only focaccia is on the menu of Liguria Bakery. Photo courtesy of Linda Esposito

Top right: The bakery has an old-fashioned feel. Photo courtesy of Kimberley Lovato

Above left: The bakery has been in North Beach since 1911. Photo courtesy of Bea D'Amico

Above right: When the focaccia is sold out, the doors are shut. Photo courtesy of Kimberley Lovato

LUCCA RAVIOLI

A taste of Italy

The smell of garlic and the Italian flags painted on the light posts in North Beach quickly give it away as San Francisco's answer to Little Italy. But what might surprise visitors, and even a few locals, is that the city's largely Latino Mission District was once a thriving neighborhood of Italian immigrants, such as the family of Michael Feno. He is the third generation to run Lucca Ravioli, an Italian grocer making fresh pasta on the same corner in the Mission since 1925.

Michael's uncle, Francesco Stangalini, opened the shop after he arrived from Lucca, Italy, in the 1920s, naming the business after his city of origin. Michael started working with his uncle and father at the shop when he was eleven years old, "sweeping behind the counter with a broom that was four inches taller than I was," he says. He graduated to stocking shelves and eventually, in the summer of 1969, Michael recalls his father telling him it was time to make the ravioli—the kind from Lucca, which are small, one-inch by one-inch squares.

Lucca Ravioli recently celebrated its ninety-second year in San Francisco. Shelves are packed with Italian products—olive oil, vinegar, jars of pepperoncinis, sweets—and cheese and salami are cut and packaged by folks who set the standard for friendly customer service. Michael says in the '60s and '70s it was mostly

> Peer through the window on Valencia Street
> and watch the pasta being made.

Top right: Lucca Ravioli has been on the same San Francisco corner since 1925. Photo courtesy of Kimberley Lovato

Above left: Lucca Ravioli is a little taste of Italy in San Francisco's Mission District. Photo courtesy of Kimberley Lovato

Above right: Fill your Italian pantry here. Photo courtesy of Kimberley Lovato

Italian families who came in to Lucca Ravioli to pick up food for holiday meals or stop by after services at the nearby Chapel of the Immaculate Conception, one of two churches in San Francisco to offer mass in Italian. Michael now welcomes San Francisco's eclectic mix of customers who appreciate quality food. Some are Italians, and many are East Coast transplants used to traditional stores like Lucca Ravioli and who want to escape to old-world Italy for a while.

1100 Valencia St.
415-647-5581
www.luccaravioli.com
Neighborhood: Mission

Authentic barbeque

If there is one phrase that sums up Memphis Minnie's and the philosophy of its founder, Bob Kantor, it is this: barbeque is *not* about the sauce. Real Southern-style barbecue gets its flavor from seasoning and the smoke generated during the essential low-and-slow cooking over burning logs or coals. Bob was insistent on it. Anything else, says his wife, Gail, is "faux-que." That's why after graduating from the California Culinary Academy, Bob traveled to Kansas City, Texas, the Carolinas, and other barbecue hotspots to soak up the nuances of what can be considered America's cuisine.

When he opened Memphis Minnie's in 1998, naming it for his mother, who hailed from Tennessee, the bar for San Francisco smokehouse barbecue was raised. Sadly, Memphis Minnie's lost Bob unexpectedly in 2013. However, the commitment to authentic smokehouse barbecue, and Bob's sense of humor, live on, thanks to Gail and longtime managers Jacki Butterfield and Tom Campbell, often seen wearing a "Memphis Minnie's: Where the Swine Is Divine" t-shirt.

The onsite meat smoker, affectionately named Olivia (a successor of Piglet, Wilbur, Porky, and Petunia), is where the smoky goodness happens, and that familiar barbeque smell tackles you when you reach the front door. Inside, checkered tablecloths peek from under

> "The biggest compliment we get is from people from the South who come in and taste our barbecue, then tell us we're doing it right."
> ~Jacki Butterfield

Top right: The swine is divine, as is the decor, at this Haight Street barbecue joint. Photo courtesy of Kimberley Lovato

Above left: Jacki Butterfield, Tom Campbell, and Gail Kantor are one happy Minnie's family. Photo courtesy of Kimberley Lovato

Above right: Meat is wood smoked for an authentic barbecue taste. Photo courtesy of Kimberley Lovato

pig drawings by neighborhood kids, and customers order from a menu that reads like Bob's personal finger-licking road map. Texas-style beef brisket cooked eighteen hours, smoked fried chicken, smoked pastrami (a nod to Bob's Brooklyn and Jewish roots), St. Louis-style ribs, Cajun andouille sausage, and fall-off-your-fork tender pulled pork all live up to Tom's t-shirt attestation.

Regulars tuck into their meals like old pros, but it's the first timers you want to watch. They bite, then stare, then slow chew and nod in what must be a Memphis Minnie's rite of passage that occurs when one has just tasted change-the-way-you-think-about-barbecue barbecue.

576 Haight St.
415-864-7675
www.memphisminnies.com
Neighborhood: Lower Haight

BOB'S DONUTS Finish the Big Donut in three minutes for a Bob's t-shirt and your name in the Hall of Fame. Photo courtesy of Kimberley Lovato

ALFRED'S STEAKHOUSE Light up dessert with tableside bananas Foster. Photo courtesy of Alanna Hale

BELCAMPO MEAT CO. Belcampo in Russian Hill is a neighborhood butcher and restaurant. Photo courtesy of Belcampo Meat Co.

CAFÉ ZOETROPE Café Zoetrope sits at the intersection of Chinatown and North Beach. Photo courtesy of Kimberley Lovato

CHINA LIVE Chinese food takes center stage. Photo Kimberley Lovato

CINDERELLA Outdoor seating has been added to invite neighbors to hang around this Russian bakery. Photo courtesy of Kimberley Lovato

COOKIE LOVE This little bakery is big on cookie love.
Photo courtesy of Kimberley Lovato

FERRY BUILDING The weekly market is one of the city's most popular. Photo courtesy of San Francisco Travel Association

GHIRARDELLI SQUARE Try Ghirardelli chocolate in its many forms. Photo courtesy of Ghirardelli Square

HANG AH TEA ROOM Soup dumplings are popular dim sum offerings. Photo courtesy of Kimberley Lovato

MINA TEST KITCHEN The MINA Test Kitchen creates a new menu and concept every three months. Photo courtesy of Kevin McCullough

SAINT FRANK COFFEE Come for a good cuppa at Saint Frank.
Photo courtesy of Michelle Park

TADICH GRILL The old-world charm of Tadich Grill makes it one of the city's most popular restaurants. Photo courtesy of Jay Singh

TAWLA A scrumptious Eastern Mediterranean spread. Photo courtesy of Tawla

THE EPICUREAN TRADER The orignal Bernal Heights shop opened in 2015. Photo courtesy of The Epicurean Trader

MENSHO TOKYO

Bowled over

In case you are wondering, the answer is yes, San Franciscans do willingly wait in line for food. It's a common sight outside many restaurants, including the thirty-seat Mensho Tokyo, a branch of Japan's most acclaimed ramen chain. Chef/owner Tomoharu Shono decided his first international outpost should be in San Francisco, he says, because of its diverse culture and for the chance to spread authentic ramen culture. Shono, as he's called, had a little help from Bay Area native and business partner Abram Plaut, who now lives and works in Japan.

Abram estimates he has eaten in more than a thousand ramen shops and has many more to go. In 2012, he met a writer for Japanese *Playboy* magazine, and their mutual ramen obsession led to a weekly column. Abram calls Shono a legit ramen master who, like a mad scientist, constantly blends, invents, tweaks, and expertly combines soup, oil, seasoning, and toppings in infinite amalgamations to create the complex flavors and surprising styles. "Anything else is pretty much just noodle soup," says Abram.

One surprise for San Francisco diners is the vegan ramen, something Abram says he was completely against at first, but Shono's blew him away. In charge of the kitchen in San Francisco is Chef Yoshi, who trained at one of Shono's shops in Japan for almost two

> "What people outside of Japan know about ramen is just the tip of the iceberg."
> ~Abram Plaut

RAMEN
Tori Paitan Ramen
Tonkotsu Ramen
Ebi Miso Ramen
Organic Ramen
Vegan Tantanmen

TSUKEMEN
Tori Paitan Gyokai Tsukemen
Spicy Ebi Miso Tsukemen

MAZESOBA
Maze Hitsuji
Vegan Mazesoba

Top right: Mensho Tokyo is popular in Japan and San Francisco. Photo courtesy of City Foodsters

Above left: Mensho's menu will please ramen fans. Photo courtesy of City Foodsters

Above right: Locals line up for delicious bowls of ramen. Photo courtesy of City Foodsters

years. Shono will also be opening a ramen school in Tokyo soon to train more chefs and other addicts like Abram. Until then, school yourself at Mensho Tokyo in San Francisco. And to answer the next question: yes, the long line is worth the wait.

672 Geary St.
415-800-8345
www.mensho.tokyo
Neighborhood: Lower Nob Hill

THE MINA TEST KITCHEN

Pop-up pleaser

Here today, gone tomorrow is bad luck for many San Francisco restaurants, but at the MINA Test Kitchen it is the norm. While the address and name stay the same, the small Marina restaurant shuts down and reopens every three to four months to relaunch a new concept and menu, keeping chef Adam Sobel on his culinary toes.

The restaurant opened in July 2015 and is both an R&D lab and a pop-up kitchen that has brought the flavors of the Middle East, India, and Italian America, among others, to the table. One of the most popular to date was the barbecue-themed International Smoke with guest chef Ayesha Curry, cookbook author and wife of Golden State Warriors basketball star Stephen Curry.

As fun as it is for guests, the rotation actually serves a purpose: to test restaurant concepts for the Mina Group and the award-winning restaurants of chef Michael Mina and potentially turn them into new brick-and-mortar locations. While it is a challenge to change up concepts and essentially create a new restaurant every few months, Adam says it is also thrilling for his team, and for guests, when it all comes together.

2120 Greenwich St.
415-625-5470
www.michaelmina.net
Neighborhood: Marina

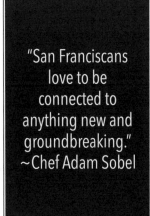

"San Franciscans love to be connected to anything new and groundbreaking."
~Chef Adam Sobel

Top: The MINA Test Kitchen chef Adam Sobel. Photo courtesy of Kevin McCullough

Bottom: The MINA Test Kitchen is located on a quiet street in the Marina. Photo courtesy of The MINA Test Kitchen

MISSION PIE

Good food—every meal, every day

It's hard not to be attracted to a place when the word "pie" is in the name, but the word "mission" is key, too, at this corner café. While it is located in the vibrant Mission District, the word also reflects the purposefulness of its mission as a business: to follow fair business practices and serve food that is healthy, affordable, and respectful to the environment.

Karen Heisler and Krystin Rubin opened Mission Pie in 2007, and it's this ethos that directs their daily menus and decisions. They buy the highest-quality ingredients, often direct from local farms, which means more money in the hands of the farmers, and they use only in-season vegetables and fruit. Thus at Mission Pie you'll see strawberry-rhubarb pie in spring, stone fruit and berry pies in summer, pumpkin pie in the fall, and apples and citrus pies for winter. What you won't find are pecans because they must travel too far, say Karen and Krystin. Mission Pie bakes instead with walnuts, grown in California only ninety miles away. Nor will you find cherries, which are labor intensive, making the end product too expensive for the diverse community of customers. What you will find is made-from-scratch, affordable food and a willingness to answer any questions about the products and food system. "Provoking the opportunity for a conversation about the food is as important as the food itself," says Karen. Mission Pie is

> "Mission Pie is an urban business with a rural food mentality."
> ~Krystin Rubin

Top left: Karen Heisler and Krystin Rubin. Photo courtesy of Kimberley Lovato

Right: Made-from-scratch wholesome food is the hallmark of Mission Pie. Photo courtesy of Kimberley Lovato

Above left: Brown cardboard boxes tied up in string. Photo courtesy of Kimberley Lovato

committed to its local community, too. It has an active internship program based on relationships with several San Francisco nonprofit agencies—interns spend four months learning transferable job and life skills. Local residents come in regularly, some daily, to order the fresh salads or small pastries, savory pot pies, or the popular "supper" that includes a choice of two daily stews served with a wholesome grain and sautéed greens for under ten dollars. Karen and Krystin say Mission Pie has become that place in the neighborhood where young and old, families and friends meet and share ideas over good food that nourishes the body and spirit.

2901 Mission St.
415-282-1500
www.missionpie.com
Neighborhood: Mission

MISTER JIU'S

Chinese star

The fabled two-story restaurant now occupied by Mister Jiu's has attracted diners almost as long as Chinatown has been around. It was Hang Fer Low before the turn of the century and then, under new ownership in 1960, became Four Seas, a popular banquet hall for Chinatown families. In fact, Mister Jiu's chef/owner, Brandon Jew, recalls attending his uncle's wedding at Four Seas as a kid. But for neighborhood outsiders, Chinatown was not a hot dining destination. It's almost poetic that when Brandon was searching for a space for his new restaurant, the Four Seas space opened up. How could he say no to serendipity?

The name Mister Jiu's is a nod to his heritage—to his grandparents, specifically—whose family name immigration officers wrote down incorrectly when they first arrived from China, changing it to Jew. The inspiration behind the restaurant is the Chinese food he knew as a child, with the goal of bringing San Franciscans back to Chinatown to dine. Brandon recalls shopping there with his grandmother, who would go from store to store, sometimes up to twelve different ones, to select the best ingredients for a meal. Seasonal, fresh, locally sourced ingredients were at the core of the meals he remembers eating as a kid, and they are brought into Mister Jiu's every day. Brandon's recipes blend classic Chinese favorites and flavors with a San Francisco twist. Think wontons made with pork from a nearby farm, sourdough scallion pancakes, and hot-and-sour soup with Dungeness crab.

Drop into the bar for housemade cocktails with names like
Happiness, Prosperity, and Wisdom.

Top left: Close-up, Brandon Jew. Photo courtesy of Kassie Borreson

Top right: Mister Jiu's looks over the heart of Chinatown. Photo courtesy of Kimberley Lovato

Above left: The dining room of Mister Jiu's. Photo courtesy of Krescent Carasso

Above right: Sign. Photo courtesy of Krescent Carasso

The kitchen is open intentionally to remove the "mystery meat" misconceptions that have tainted Chinese food's reputation, while the dining room is as contemporary as the cuisine, though the teak tables do bear a beloved old Chinese restaurant mainstay: the lazy Susan. After only six months in business, Mister Jiu's received a Michelin star, and curious diners are coming back to Chinatown. You could call Brandon a culinary ambassador for the neighborhood. Someone has to be. "The next generation needs to celebrate great Chinese cuisine and its history," he says.

28 Waverly Place
415-857-9688
www.misterjius.com
Neighborhood: Chinatown

MITCHELL'S ICE CREAM

Sweet history

Stare at the apartment building that houses Mitchell's Ice Cream and you won't notice anything peculiar. Even the line spilling out the front door is normal on a hot day. But prior to the Mitchell family opening its popular parlor in 1953, the City of San Francisco had decided to widen San Jose Avenue and planned to raze this very building. The Mitchell family, who had built the edifice in 1912 and still owns it today, fought to save it. In an epic compromise, the city agreed to keep the building but lift it up and turn it sideways, making room for its road. Needless to say, the liquor store that had existed on the ground floor was vacated for the project, and the space remained empty for years. Larry Mitchell and his brother, Jack, were go-getters, keen to start their own business. They decided on ice cream and taught themselves how to make it. With the help of their father and uncles, they built the store by hand. Mitchell's opened in June of 1953. Today Larry's daughter, Linda, and her brother, Brian, run the show. During the 1960s, when vanilla, strawberry, and chocolate were the norm, Mitchell's introduced mango to the Bay Area, along with other exotic flavors, using imported fruit from the Philippines and Latin America. Mango is still the number-one seller, says Linda, but there are forty different flavors, made each day, some created by Brian, while others have come from customer

> "When I was an auditor, no one wanted to see me.
> Now people are happy when they see me."
> ~Linda Mitchell

Top left: A lineup of tropical and traditional treats. Photo courtesy of Mitchell's Ice Cream

Top Right: Expect a crowd on a hot day. Photo courtesy of Mitchell's Ice Cream

Above left: There's something for every taste bud on the menu. Photo courtesy of Mitchell's Ice Cream

Above right: Mitchell's has been a neighborhood hangout since 1953. Photo courtesy of Mitchell's Ice Cream

and employee suggestions. The neighborhood ice cream shop has been around for more than sixty years now, and Linda says many of its employees are the neighborhood kids who came in with their parents. It's like one big happy family, she says. Driven by an entrepreneurial spirit, quality, and customer service, it is also one of San Francisco's sweetest landmarks.

688 San Jose Ave.
415-648-2300
www.mitchellsicecream.com
Neighborhood: Bernal Heights/Outer Mission

NOPALITO

Seasoned with respect

The story of how Nopalito got its start swirls around San Francisco like a plume of fog. At Nopa, one of San Francisco's busiest and most popular neighborhood restaurants, Gonzalo Guzman and another cook, José Ramos, were often tasked with preparing the evening "family meal," the repast made for the staff before opening.

The food inspired co-owners Jeff Hanak, Allyson Jossel, and chef Laurence Jossel to give Gonzalo and José their own stage and call it Nopalito (little Nopa), a place where their high-quality Mexican food and recipes would simmer and shine. Allyson confirms there is some validity to the tale but says the story goes a little deeper. Gonzalo and Laurence had had a long history of working together. Pure talent didn't hurt either, she says. "Gonzalo is one of the most motivated, determined, and committed people I have ever worked with." The mutual respect is shared. Gonzalo says he is beyond touched and owes a special thanks to Laurence, an accomplished chef with an impressive San Francisco resume who pushed Gonzalo to do things he never thought he could do.

Nopalito opened in 2009 and is held to the same exacting standards as the acclaimed Nopa. While the menu started mostly with family recipes from Gonzalo and his co-chef at that time, Gonzalo mans the kitchen alone now, presenting recipes from his heritage with fresh California ingredients in the best way possible.

> Nopalito doesn't take reservations, but it has a call-ahead waitlist and will send you a text.

Top: Making tortillas. Photo courtesy of Nopalito

Above left: Gonzalo Guzman. Photo courtesy of Nopalito

Above center: Nopalito has two locations in San Francisco. Photo courtesy of Bea D'Amico

Above right: Nopalito's Broderick Street dining room. Photo courtesy of Bea D'Amico

Some of the must-try items, he says, are the empanadas, panuchos, pozole, and caldo tlalpeño (a spicy Mexican chicken soup). One thing is clear: he puts his heart into every dish, which makes returning a love-at-first-bite moment again and again. That's the thing about love. Offer it unconditionally and, like good seasoning, it enriches whatever and whomever it touches.

306 Broderick St.
415-535-3969
www.nopalitosf.com
Neighborhood: Lower Haight/NoPa

OFF THE GRID

A little night market

Like most cities, San Francisco embraced the food truck phenomenon with open arms and mouths. Matt Cohen took things to the next level and launched his gathering of food trucks, called Off the Grid, in 2010, inspired by evening markets and fireworks festivals he'd experienced in Japan while teaching English. He says he wanted to emulate the vibrancy that permeated those social events.

Seven years later, with more than fifty weekly locations around the Bay Area, Matt and Off the Grid have succeeded, big time. Friday night's Off the Grid at Fort Mason Center is held March through October and is the largest night market in San Francisco, with more than a dozen varied food trucks, open-air kitchen vendors, several bars, and live entertainment that lure people to gather under strings of lights and mingle with strangers and friends.

Matt says Off the Grid has evolved from a food truck stop into a reflection of San Francisco itself: diverse, creative, and progressive. But the first priority is always to make sure people have a great time and, as he did in Japan, experience community in an exceptional setting.

Fort Mason Center
2 Marina Blvd.
415-339-5888
www.offthegridsf.com
Neighborhood: Marina

Top: The night markets of Asia inspired founder Matt Cohen's vision at Fort Mason. Photo courtesy of Gamma Nine

Above left: Off the Grid cohosts the family-friendly Presidio Picnic with the Presidio Trust. Photo courtesy of Gamma Nine

Above right: Yoga enthusiasts at Off the Grid's Presidio Picnic. Photo courtesy of Kimberley Lovato

Presidio Picnic, sponsored by Off the Grid and Presidio Trust, is a popular event held on spring and summer Sundays in the Presidio.

THE OLD CLAM HOUSE

The little restaurant that could

At the time The Old Clam House opened its doors in 1861, Abraham Lincoln was still the president of the United States, and the restaurant was waterfront property. The population of San Francisco then was a whopping sixty thousand people. At 156 years and counting, The Old Clam House has the distinction of being the oldest restaurant in San Francisco operating in the same location.

Admittedly, the address is not a convenient one, folded into an industrial area, and it is no longer waterfront. It is just out of the way enough that most probably don't know it exists or have forgotten that it does. The silver lining is that it is on the way to and from the airport and worth a stop for a taste of San Francisco nostalgia. Originally known as the Oakdale Bar & Clam House, the restaurant has changed hands and names multiple times.

When local businessman Jerry Dal Bozzo bought The Old Clam House in 2011, he says it was in a terrible state of disrepair and had been converted in the 1980s to an *American Graffiti*-esque diner, complete with hubcaps and license plates on the walls and an old Jaguar behind the bar.

It was the historical value of the place that prompted Jerry to get involved. He didn't want to see it disappear from San Francisco. He salvaged the stamped copper ceiling and checkerboard tile floors. He added wainscoting, wallpaper, and historical photos. In the attic Jerry found a set of old windows with square nails still holding

All diners are served a shot of cloudy clam broth, a tradition that started when the restaurant opened.

Top left: A clam bake in a pot is big enough for two. Photo courtesy of Misha Bruk

Top right: The enclosed patio features old windows found in the attic. Photo courtesy of Misha Bruk

Above: The Old Clam House exterior. Photo courtesy of Misha Bruk

them together, and he placed them between the dining room and the enclosed patio. The floors and ceilings of the resilient restaurant slope, and the feeling of a Gold Rush-era saloon permeates the unpretentious bar. The menu is seafood heavy, with specialties such as thick clam chowder in a bread bowl, whole roasted Dungeness crab in garlic sauce, and the signature clam bake cioppino, a generous heap of clams, mussels, crab, shrimp, calamari, fish fillet, and vegetables in a tangy red sauce.

299 Bayshore Blvd.
415-826-4880
www.theoldclamhousesf.com
Neighborhood: Bayview/Hunters Point

ORIGINAL JOE'S

A family affair

The roots of Original Joe's run as deep as the pylons of the Golden Gate Bridge. In fact, both local landmarks opened the same year, in 1937. One was painted "International Orange" and spans the mouth of the San Francisco Bay, while the other was a fourteen-stool counter on Taylor Street serving classic Croatian-Italian-American comfort food prepared by Tony Rodin, an immigrant in search of the American Dream. Eighty years on, both the bridge and Original Joe's still serve up a sense of old San Francisco.

Tony eventually handed his spatula over to his daughter and son-in-law, Marie and John J. Duggan, whose own son and daughter, Elena Duggan and John Duggan, are now also entwined in the three-generation family business. Unfortunately, a fire destroyed the Taylor Street location in 2007. But just five years later, Original Joe's swung open its doors in North Beach, taking over a corner spot facing Saints Peter and Paul Church. The transition was tough for the family, as they had to let go of memories tied to the former address, especially for Marie, who didn't set foot in the new restaurant until it opened. When she finally did, the family matriarch cried with joy, recall Elena and John. One reason, perhaps, is that Original Joe's gives the impression of having been around forever. John and Elena point to their family history weaved into every

> "I never tire of the pride I feel as part of the tradition my grandfather started."
> ~John Duggan

Top right: An entire wall is dedicated to Original Joe's history. Photo courtesy of Kimberley Lovato

Above left: Original Joe's is on a popular North Beach corner. Photo courtesy of Eric Wolfinger

Above right: The Duggan family. Photo courtesy of Eric Wolfinger

corner. The red booths, salvaged from the old restaurant, were re-covered and now flank the main dining room; some wood paneling and fireplace bricks were part of the old bar; family photos, letters from local government officials, and memorabilia string along an entire wall; and the menu is dotted with house specialties such as eggplant parmigiana and Joe's meatballs made using Tony's original recipes. But it's the counter stools saved in the fire and brought over from Taylor Street that are in a position of honor, in front of the teeming new kitchen—a reminder that at the heart of Original Joe's is family.

601 Union St.
415-775-4877
www.originaljoessf.com
Neighborhood: North Beach/Telegraph Hill

PIER 23

Musical watering hole

Check the boxes for live music, good drinks, and waterfront dining, and Pier 23 is one of the few places left at the top of the list. The unassuming clapboard shack with the simple neon sign sits squat on the Embarcadero between the Ferry Building and Fisherman's Wharf, and it has been owned and operated by the same family for more than thirty years. Its history, however, goes back another four decades. What has remained consistent for San Franciscans is Pier 23's reputation as a low-key local watering hole with strong drinks and amazing live music.

When Flicka McGurrin took over with her business partner, Peggy Knickerbocker, it was obvious that food had not been a priority for a while. At best, guests could grab a squished hamburger or a grilled-cheese sandwich. But given that Flicka and Peggy had been sought-after caterers prior to their Pier 23 debut, things took a turn for the delicious. They expanded the menu, as well as the opening hours, making it a lunch and dinner restaurant.

Flicka now runs the business with her son, Mac. Business crowds fill the tables mid-week, while weekends, especially sunny ones, mean locals clamoring for a seat on the back patio to devour oysters, Dungeness crab, grilled fish tacos, and a much better burger. Music is still the main event at Pier 23, says Flicka, who has a deep bench of talent. She gets many local favorites asking to come and play, as well

> " We really haven't changed the place much.
> We are what we are."
> ~Flicka McGurrin

Top: The small hut on the water has been a hot spot for decades. Photo courtesy of Pier 23

Above left: The waterside back patio is popular on sunny days. Photo courtesy of Pier 23

Above right: Fresh fish tacos. Photo courtesy of Pier 23

as international musicians such as Australian pianist Pugsley Buzzard, who drops by Pier 23 when he tours the United States, and Luis Coloma from Spain, whose music Flicka describes as "some badass boogie-woogie." You might also catch Latin jazz, funk rock, R&B, surf groove, reggae, and any combination thereof because there is music almost every night of the week, keeping Pier 23 a favorite local hangout that has only changed for the better.

415-362-5125
www.pier23cafe.com
Neighborhood: Embarcadero

RED'S JAVA HOUSE

The more things change

In a town like San Francisco, where organic foods, gluten-free diets, and juice cleanses are as popular as wearing leggings as pants, Red's Java House is proudly *not* that place. You won't get pretty food posed on plates. In fact, you won't get a plate at all, and there will definitely not be organic lettuce and tomato on your sourdough-swaddled burger. Red's looks its shun-the-new part, too, leaning lopsided against the edge of Pier 30 almost underneath the Bay Bridge. Inside, pale yellow paint flakes if you pick it, and the round stools look like withered mushrooms that will topple should you dare to sit on them. Back in the 1930s, it was called Franco's Lunch and was a haunt for longshoremen working on San Francisco's waterfront, where a young newsboy named Tom "Red" McGarvey—a redhead— also worked selling copies of the local paper. In 1955, along with his brother Mike, Red bought Franco's and christened it with its new ruby name. With only a few exceptions, that's about all that appears to have changed since. At the suggestion of her father, who worked at the Port of San Francisco, current owner Tiffany Pisoni purchased Red's in 2009 from the husband-and-wife team who had bought the place from the McGarvey brothers in 1990. She says it didn't take long for loyal customers to critique her "drastic" changes. Tiffany removed piles of junk from the back patio; she discarded the non-working coffee-roasting equipment hogging the corner of the dining

> "Red's is all about its customers. It's a true San Francisco place where everyone is welcome."
> ~Tiffany Pisoni

Q: What name is given to the darkest part of shadow cast by the earth or moon during an eclipse?

Hamburger or Hot Dog	$5.53 +TAX
Double Burger or Double Dog	$7.97 +TAX
Cheeseburger or Cheesedog	$5.92 +TAX
Double Cheeseburger or Double Cheesedog	$8.73 TAX
Chili Cheeseburger	$5.85 +TAX

We Don't Serve Lettuce or Tomato

Combos

Double Cheeseburger & Soda	$11.90 +TAX
Double Cheeseburger, Fries & Soda	$13.33 +TAX
Hamburger or Hot Dog & Beer	$9.53 +TAX
Single Cheeseburger & Soda	$7.90 +TAX
Double Cheeseburger & Bud	$12.90 +TAX
Double Cheeseburger, Fries & Lagunitas IPA	$16.21 +TAX

Top right: Burgers are served on sourdough rolls at Red's. Photo courtesy of Kimberley Lovato

Above left: All smiles behind the counter at Red's, unless you order lettuce and tomato on your burger. Photo courtesy of Kimberley Lovato

Above right: Tiffany Pisoni purchased Red's in 2009 at the suggestion of her father, who worked at the Port of San Francisco. Photo courtesy of Kimberley Lovato

area; she repainted the walls, using a paint chip to match the exact color; and, gasp, she dared to move a mop from its visible position into a closet, and customers noticed. Those things make Tiffany laugh now, she says, because they make Red's the rare kind of place where people care enough to make sure it doesn't change with the times. Tiffany did add a website and internet, though. The dial-up connection couldn't keep up with credit card processing technology. But don't ask for a Wi-Fi code lest you receive the same response you'll get if you ask for lettuce and tomato on your burger.

Pier 30
415-777-5626
www.redsjavahouse.com
Neighborhood: Embarcadero

SAINT FRANK COFFEE

More than a cuppa

Kevin Bohlin came to San Francisco in 2010 with coffee on his mind. The owner of Saint Frank on Russian Hill had just finished his short stint as a middle school art teacher in Texas, where, during grad school, he had taken a part-time job as a barista. This planted the seed for an obsession.

Kevin entered a barista training program and moved to San Francisco, where he took a job with Ritual Coffee. During his tenure, he entered the US Barista Championship in 2011 and came in sixth (of 150), solidifying his place in San Francisco's high-octane coffee culture. Interested in furthering his bean education, Kevin began accompanying Ritual on buying trips to countries such as Costa Rica, Guatemala, and Honduras. Kevin says it was while traveling to these beautiful locations that he discovered the unique community that coffee growers belong to. "Getting to know them and see how hard they work was transformative," he says. Kevin decided to begin a coffee brand of his own. He called it Saint Frank, for San Francisco, to have a connection to the community. It's also a derivative of the name of Saint Francis of Assisi, a man of action who gave up a life of luxury to devote himself to Christianity.

That message is a powerful one to Kevin, and he draws a parallel with offering coffee drinkers a tasty cup of joe while also, hopefully, offering a deeper connection to the people behind it. Saint Frank

> "At Saint Frank, coffee is about more than just the coffee."
> ~Kevin Bohlin

Top right: Saint Frank Coffee is a neighborhood favorite. Photo courtesy of Michelle Park

Above left: Kevin Bohlin with one of his coffee partners in Thailand. Photo courtesy of Michelle Park

Above right: Saint Frank is a popular Russian Hill hangout. Photo courtesy of Bea D'Amico

opened in 2013. The minimalist café is a social hub, the way a neighborhood coffee shop should be, he says, but Kevin still travels every few months to meet his producers, people he proudly calls his friends. On the shelves at Saint Frank are bags of beans accompanied by cards that provide tasting notes and background information on the farm and people that grew the beans. In each cup, a devotion to that community is poured.

2340 Polk St.
415-775-1619
www.saintfrankcoffee.com
Neighborhood: Russian Hill

SAM'S GRILL & SEAFOOD RESTAURANT

Grand Sam

In the rough-and-tumble world of restaurant openings and closings in San Francisco, it's nice to find longtime haunts still sticking it out, especially ones saved by devoted patrons. Opened as an oyster saloon called M. B. Moraghan's in 1867, Sam's, took its name from the next proprietor, Sam Zenovich. Though he called his restaurant the Reception Café, everyone else called it Sam's, and the name stuck, even after it changed hands and addresses a few more times. The proprietor and managing partner these days is Peter Quartaroli, who has worked at Sam's off and on for more than twenty-five years, filling in as a waiter or maitre d' when he came back to town. He knew the Seput family, who had purchased the restaurant from Sam and ran it for two generations. And he knew Phil Lyons, the following owner, who wanted to retire.

In 2014, a group of regulars and investors took a leap and saved the downtown landmark from sure extinction. "I was fortunate to get tremendous support from a very loyal group of customers, friends, and staff. We are thrilled that we were able to save Sam's and once again have a thriving San Francisco institution," says Peter. Not much has changed in terms of overall vibe. The lunchtime martini

Sam's opened a heated patio, called Sam's Seafood Alley, adjacent to the restaurant in 2015.

Left: The team of Sam's welcomes you. Photo courtesy of Sam's Grill

Right: Downtown favorite. Photo courtesy of Sam's Grill

and manhattan are still as popular as the beloved wood-paneled booths with privacy curtains, and regulars are still welcomed by name. Peter says he cleaned the place up and simplified the menu, focusing on quality and execution, while keeping Sam's classics front and center. That means you can still order petrale sole or sand dabs, as well as only-in-San Francisco specialties such as cioppino and Hangtown fry.

When Peter is not at Sam's, he works in the film industry, and he even wrote a film script set at Sam's. Though it hasn't been made yet, it's called *Tony's Money* and is based on a real person who worked at Sam's for more than forty years. Here's hoping we see Tony on the silver screen soon and the bright lights of grand old Sam's welcoming San Franciscans for another 150 years.

374 Bush St.
415-421-0594
www.samsgrillsf.com
Neighborhood: Financial District

SAN FRANCISCO HERB CO.

Herbs and spice, and everything nice

An entire store dedicated to herbs, spices, teas, and botanicals at rock bottom prices? That sounds par for the course in San Francisco, where food, its accoutrements, and democratic principles live in symbiotic bliss.

Neil Hanscomb is the owner, and he calls himself a numbers guy, though these days you might see him reconciling with the strong currents while windsurfing off Crissy Field. He was working as a CPA in the early 1970s when the herb business came up for sale. Neil jumped in, and ten years later he bought a small storefront with an adjacent warehouse on Fourteenth Street. Back then it wasn't the prime real estate it is today, and he gets offers all the time to buy the space that takes up one-sixth of a city block. Inside are rows and shelves of local and imported, common and unusual herbs, essential oils, botanicals, roots and berries, extracts and culinary spices, and more. Perhaps that's why his client list includes some of the Bay Area's top chefs, craft brewers, and distillers, such as Distillery No. 209, which crafts gin and vodka near AT&T Park. Neil says he gets discovered one customer at a time and is always astonished when they find him. "I don't advertise. People want value, not fluff."

250 Fourteenth St.
415-861-7174
www.sfherb.com
Neighborhood: Mission

Trends in herbs and spices come and go, but catnip has been a steady best seller for decades. Meow.

162

Top left: Neil Hanscomb, avid windsurfer and owner of San Francisco Herb Co. Photo courtesy of San Francisco Herb Co.

Top right: Your source for herbs of all kinds. Photo courtesy of Bea D'Amico

Above: Variety is the spice of life. Photo courtesy of Bea D'Amico

SAN FRANCISCO PICKLE COMPANY

Not your average pickle

Ideas are often born out of necessity—or cravings, when it comes to pickles. That's how Chris Williams had his light bulb moment, which sparked while scouring grocery store aisles for piquant pickles.

The Boston transplant (and admitted spicy food addict) graduated from Le Cordon Bleu San Francisco but says he never intended to work in a restaurant. Though he did cater for a stint, he has spent the past seven years growing his pickle company. His culinary expertise comes in handy, and Chris has created eighteen different flavors, all made with 100 percent natural ingredients sourced from local farmers markets and aged in a brine of herbs and spices.

He's a one-man show in a commercial kitchen in the Hunter's Point neighborhood, and he hand labels every jar, too. His pickles are sold online and around San Francisco, in stores such as Hot Lix on Pier 39 and at Village Market in the Ferry Building. For spice fanatics he suggests the "Dragon's Breath," a not-for-the-faint-of-heart medley of ghost, habanero, and serrano peppers. For more sensitive taste buds, the "Simon and Garpickle," made with parsley, sage, rosemary, and thyme, really sings.

www.sfpickleco.com

> "My brine makes a good marinade for chicken, too."
> ~Chris Williams

Top right: San Francisco's skyline is on every jar. Photo courtesy of San Francisco Pickle Co.

Above left: Spike your pantry with piquant pickles. Photo courtesy of Kimberley Lovato

Above right: Chris Williams. Photo courtesy of Kimberley Lovato

SCHUBERT'S BAKERY

Let them eat Fuerst Pueckler

For those in search of high-quality, special occasion cakes reminiscent of an old-world bakery, Schubert's is the go-to. German immigrant Oswald R. Schubert built the original bakery on Fillmore Street in 1911 before moving it to its current location in the 1940s. Brothers Ralph and Lutz Wenzel now man the spatula. Also German and hailing from a baking family, the duo had careers as pastry chefs in Europe and the Middle East before coming to America. They were working at Schubert's when owners Hilmar and Annie Maier, who had purchased the bakery from Oswald Schubert, decided to retire in 1995.

Ralph and Lutz proudly continue the tradition. Their pride shows in every handmade flower, swirl, and delicate chocolate leaf bedecking their opera, mango mousse, and famous Swedish princess cakes. If you want a Fuerst Pueckler cake, formerly known as a Neopolitan, then look no further. This hard-to-find pastry masterpiece of white and chocolate cake, chocolate and raspberry whipped cream, and chocolate ganache has been Schubert's original since 1911, which is why the German bakery remains one of a kind, even more than 105 years later.

521 Clement St.
415-752-1580
www.schuberts-bakery.com
Neighborhood: Inner Richmond

166

Top right: Each cake is a piece of art. Photo courtesy of Kimberley Lovato

Above left: Order cakes for pick-up or have a slice on the spot. Photo courtesy of Kimberley Lovato

Above right: The bakery case is filled with sweet delights. Photo courtesy of Kimberley Lovato

SoMa strEAT FOOD PARK

Meet-and-eat street

Walk around any city these days and you're likely to stumble upon a food truck dishing out anything from kimchi to crème brûlée. San Francisco is no exception when it comes to hungry residents circling these modern chuck wagons like seagulls around the bay. However, San Francisco native Carlos Muela capitalized on the mad love for these rolling restaurants by creating the city's first permanent address for food trucks. Though he never wanted to run a food truck himself, Carlos worked in his parents' two Spanish restaurants, which opened in San Francisco's Mission District long before the neighborhood became the bread and butter of San Francisco real estate brokers. He has always loved the concept of a tapas-style communal eating place. When he graduated from college, Carlos, along with his father, spitballed an idea for an urban version that would stand up to San Francisco's savvy palate and feed its unpretentious sensibilities. SoMa StrEAT Food Park opened in 2012 and is now a must-visit mash-up of beer garden, community kitchen, and special event space (check out Trivia Night every Tuesday) that welcomes people seven days a week to sit at picnic tables under strings of Edison bulbs and nibble from a rotating fleet of food trucks. A festival atmosphere radiates on nights when live bands play or on game days when fans watch the Giants or the 49ers on large TV screens. When Carlos thinks about his success now,

> "The biggest risk, my biggest fear, was whether we were going to get tenants and customers to show up at this location."
> ~Carlos Muela

Top right: Concerts contribute to a lively atmosphere. Photo courtesy of SoMa StrEAT Food Park

Above left: Carlos Muela opened his second food truck park, called Spark Social, in Mission Bay in 2016. Photo courtesy of Kimberley Lovato

Above right: Lunch hour crowds are spoiled by a good variety of food trucks. Photo courtesy of SoMa StrEAT Food Park

he seems relaxed, though he admits the concept was risky from the get-go given the location: a vacant lot, under a freeway, with no foot traffic to speak of. But that's the thing about a great idea—it isn't one until someone makes it one and leaves the rest of us to wonder how we ever food trucked before SoMa StrEAT Food Park rolled into town.

428 Eleventh St.
www.somastreatfoodpark.com
Neighborhood: SoMa

SONG TEA & CERAMICS

A clean, well-lit place for tea

Peer in the window here and it looks like a hip ceramics gallery—a minimalist, airy space with cement floors, where handiwork is lined up on floating shelves and displayed on mid-century-modern tables. At closer glance, however, it is a tea-tasting room where Peter Luong, owner and peripatetic tea buyer, puts a modern and accessible face on China's ancient tea tradition.

Peter grew up in San Francisco, where his parents owned a Chinese apothecary. After working in the tech industry, and after the dot-com bust of 2003, Peter joined the family business and helped turn it into the well-known Red Blossom Tea Company in Chinatown, where he was a tea buyer for twelve years.

In 2014 he opened Song Tea with a mission to demystify tea and bring attention to its complexities and possibilities. Peter says tea is where wine was twenty years ago and should be looked at much the same way in terms of the plant, terroir, and skill needed for producing a quality product.

He travels about twice a year to growing regions of China and Taiwan to source green, white, black, and oolong teas from growers who value tradition and craftsmanship. Song Tea stocks a maximum of thirty teas at any given time, which are sold in small quantities and rotated out often. Some are different and rare, which Peter says he buys not for the sake of the strange but because they are good. Set up

> "The absence of knowledge makes tea somewhat mystical, but there is actually a lot of hard work that goes into tea."
> ~Peter Luong

170

Top right: Song Tea pays homage to tea. Photo courtesy of Bea D'Amico

Above left: Peter Luong in his tea gallery and tasting room. Photo courtesy of Kimberley Lovato

Above right: The tea room is tucked into lower Pacific Heights. Photo courtesy of Bea D'Amico

a tasting at Song Tea, and you'll be treated to a ceremony of sorts led by Peter or a staff member, who will leave you convinced that tea, like wine and the people who make it, also has a deep and layered story to tell. It turns out that the ceramics are not just objets d'art, either. They are carefully selected by Peter, too.

As glasses do with wine, these vessels enhance the tea's flavor. That they clink and tinkle as Peter scoops, steeps, and pours his fine brews creates an experience that is more like an opus than a song for tea lovers.

2120 Sutter St.
415-885-2118
www.songtea.com
Neighborhood: Lower Pacific Heights

SOURDOUGH BREAD

Weird science

For years it was thought that San Francisco was the only place on the planet where sourdough bread could be made because of a specific type of bacteria found in our foggy air. Locals love a good San Francisco-created-the-world story. But this friendly bacteria, called *lactobacillus sanfranciscensis*, is found everywhere. Good sourdough comes down to science, along with technique, patience, and the starter—a mixture of flour, water, wild yeast, and bacteria, which is added to fresh dough and permeates the finished product with its characteristic tang. The myriad talented bakers around the city knead (get it?) no introduction, and researching your preferred sourdough is a tasty San Francisco must do.

Try it.

Tartine Bakery is a James Beard Award-winning bakery with legendary lineups for the impeccable bread.
600 Guerrero St.
415-487-2600
www.tartinebakery.com

Boudin Bakery is the granddaddy of sourdough, and its factory tour takes you behind the scenes.
160 Jefferson St.
415-928-1849
www.boudinbakery.com

Sour Flour teaches workshops on making your own sourdough bread so you never have to go without.
2937 Twenty-Fourth St.
650-868-0243
www.sourflour.org

What is Sourdough?

Ever since 1849, we have been baking San Francisco Sourdough according to the Boudin family's time-honored methods. Our secret: the mother dough, an ancient method of making bread rise using only the wild yeast present in the local environment, "caught" from the air and cultivated with a mixture of water and flour. Surviving only in our fog-cooled climate, our mother dough imparts a flavor and texture unlike any other bre____ _ world.

#BO____KERY

Top left: Boudin Bakery Museum. Photo courtesy of Kimberley Lovato

Top right: Boudin's bakers are on display. Photo courtesy of Kimberley Lovato

Above left: Josey Baker Bread is all sourdough, all the time. Photo courtesy of Kimberley Lovato

Above right: Learn to make bread at Sour Flour. Photo courtesy of Sour Flour

STARBELLY

Patio picnics

If you love a good picnic but prefer to skip the grass, the ants, San Francisco's cold summer weather, and the cooking, say hello to Starbelly.

The friendly Castro bistro is beloved for its craft brews and healthy and hearty home-style brunch, lunch, and dinner menus, but the secret star of Starbelly is the quarterly patio picnic. The ticketed event transforms the covered wooden deck into a family-style supper complete with strings of lights, overflowing planter boxes, colorful cloth napkins, and picnic tables. Meals are prepared by executive chef Adam Timney, who selects a different main course for each picnic. Honey-glazed ribs, Santa Maria tri-tip, fried chicken, and even whole-roasted hog have made an appearance. December is always Dungeness crab (this is San Francisco, after all).

Adam says he started the picnics to showcase the back patio, but over time Starbelly picnics have morphed into a place where neighbors and friends gather to slow down and reconnect.

3583 Sixteenth St.
415-252-7500
www.starbellysf.com
Neighborhood: Castro

"Our hope is to build a sense of community."
~Adam Timney

Top right: Neighbors love the quarterly patio picnics at Starbelly. Photo courtesy of Blake Young

Above left: Executive chef Adam Timney goes whole hog. Photo courtesy of Blake Young

Above right: Starbelly's covered deck turns into a popular patio picnic. Photo courtesy of Declan Mckerr

SWAN OYSTER DEPOT

A seafaring favorite

There are two things you will notice the first time you come to Swan Oyster Depot: there is always a line out the door, even before it opens at 10:30 a.m., and you feel instantly welcome.

The wholesale fish market, originally called Cable Oyster Depot, was opened by the Lausten brothers around the turn of the century, and they used a horse-drawn carriage to deliver their seafood throughout San Francisco. When the place burned down after the 1906 earthquake, it reopened on Polk Street, where it has been since 1912. The Danish brothers sold the business in 1946 to Sal Sancimino and family, who have run the business ever since. Despite the change of hands and name, the friendly vibe and commitment to fresh fish (and fresh sass) live on. Behind the narrow, eighteen-stool counter, Kevin Sancimino jokes with a customer who walks in for an early pick-up order, while a coterie of employees made up of family and friends jostle bins of oysters and clams and fill the window with whole fish, crab, and other seafood to woo passersby, not that they'll need any convincing.

The hundred-plus-year-old fish market and restaurant might be tiny, but it is big on reputation, one built entirely on word of mouth. It continues to be a favorite of locals, tourists, and even celebrities, such as Bing Crosby, who once dined here, and Anthony Bourdain, who cracked crab and jokes at Swan Oyster Depot in 2015. Once

Despite the rogue websites that sporadically appear online, Swan Oyster Depot has none, and the owners plan to keep it that way.

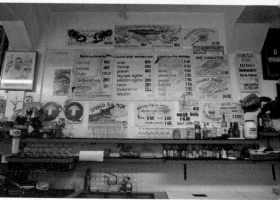

Top right: A line out the door is a regular sight. Photo courtesy of Kimberley Lovato

Above left: Kevin Sancimino makes everyone feel welcome. Photo courtesy of Kimberley Lovato

Above right: The menu at Swan Oyster Depot. Photo courtesy of Kimberley Lovato

inside, you sit elbow to elbow on stools and order from a menu board that includes chowders, salads, oysters, fish, and the best seller—the combo salad with bay shrimp, prawns, and a dollop of Dungeness crab meat on a bed of lettuce, drizzled in creamy Louie dressing.

People might come for the best seafood in the city, but they return for Swan Oyster Depot's warm welcome, also delivered fresh daily. Kevin says he loves that people wait, but his focus is on the person sitting in front of him and the Swan Oyster Depot motto: no one is ever a stranger here.

1517 Polk St.
415-673-1101
Neighborhood: Polk Gulch

THE TACO SHOP @ UNDERDOGS

Nick's way

With a full bar, half a dozen flat-screen TVs, and team memorabilia dangling from the ceiling, Underdogs has all the trappings of a great sports bar. But there is an added bonus tucked inside: a taco shop.

If you've been in San Francisco for some time, you've heard of Nick's Crispy Tacos on Polk Street. The big reveal, however, is that Nick Fasanella, the Nick in the name, hasn't been there since 2006. It's a long, sad, and not very honorable story, he says, but rest assured—the real Nick, and his tacos made "Nick's way," are alive and well. Nick's way means a grilled crispy corn tortilla wrapped in a soft tortilla, with a choice of meat or fish, Monterey Jack cheese, pinto beans, pico de gallo, and a generous dollop of guacamole. This from a guy who grew up in Connecticut with little taco interaction. But Nick loved food, and after graduating from The Culinary Institute of America and working in some highfalutin restaurants, he ditched the starch whites for flip-flops and set sail as a chef on private yachts for seven years, traveling all over the world, including Mexico, where he says he fell in love with the cuisine.

In 1999 he hopped on his motorcycle in Miami and two-wheeled it to San Francisco, a town that knows a thing or two about tacos, and became a regular at La Taqueria in the Mission. When offered the

Check out Nick's other eatery, TACKO, in the Marina. The A-C-K in the name are Nantucket Airport's call letters.

178

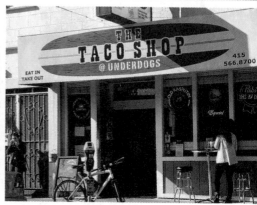

Top left: Nick Fasanella is *the* Nick behind Nick's Crispy Tacos. Photo courtesy of Kimberley Lovato

Top right: "Nick's way" tacos are made with both a soft and a hard shell. Photo courtesy of Underdogs

Above left: A sports bar with a hidden surprise—Nick's Crispy Tacos. Photo courtesy of Underdogs

Above right: Underdogs is a sports bar with a beachy vibe. Photo courtesy of Kimberley Lovato

chance to open his own space, he did it inside a nightclub on Polk Street and called it Nick's Crispy Tacos. After his unceremonious ouster, friend and bar owner Doug Marschke invited Nick to bring his customers (and his tacos) to Underdogs. The Taco Shop @ Underdogs was born in 2008. Nick and Doug are often there, too. Nick, the smiling face, and Doug, the operations guy, chat up neighbors who seem genuinely happy that Nick and Nick's way have found their way to a laid-back sports bar in the cool corner of the city.

1824 Irving St.
415-566-8700
www.tacoshopsf.com
Neighborhood: Outer Sunset

TADICH GRILL

The quintessential classic

Trendy is not what you'd call a 158-year-old restaurant with wood paneling and waiters wrapped in white aprons, but there is novelty to the classics in San Francisco, and Tadich Grill is the quintessential classic. Considered the city's oldest restaurant, it can trace its origins back to the Gold Rush era and a coffee tent set up by Croatian immigrants on Long Wharf. The name of the place and its address changed over the decades, but the grill's elevation to legendary status really took root in 1912, when another Croatian named John Tadich gave the restaurant its current name and delighted patrons with excellent seafood and days-of-yore stories that kept them coming back. In 1928, three brothers named Buich took over, and Tadich Grill has been in the family ever since.

Tadich Grill is packed day and night, despite the hard-line no-reservations policy. General manager David Hanna says this keeps things fair. Judging by the guest book, in which names such as Johnny Carson, Tim Burton, Arnold Schwarzenegger, and Joe Montana are scrawled, even the who's who are just like you and me when it comes to grabbing a table. The late and beloved *Chronicle* columnist Herb Caen was also a frequent visitor. There's a martini named after him at the bar, made with vodka or, as he called it, Vitamin V.

The food at Tadich Grill is as consistent as its place in San Franciscans' hearts. No need to tinker with the fried sand dabs or crab

> "We all feel like this is our baby, and we take great care of it. If we get a complaint, it really hurts."
> ~David Hanna

Top left: Tadich Grill is almost as old as San Francisco itself. Photo courtesy of Jay Singh

Top right: The no-reservations restaurant is jam-packed every day of the week. Photo courtesy of Jay Singh

Above left: Tadich Grill is San Francisco's ultimate classic. Photo courtesy of Bryan Kitch

Above right: The cioppino is the restaurant's best seller. Photo courtesy of Jay Singh

Louie. The Hangtown fry is fine the way it has been since day one. The cioppino is the most popular dish on the menu, with more than twenty thousand bowls served each year. Yes, people continue to come to Tadich Grill, says David, because the food is good and the service is friendly. They know what they're getting, and that is a taste of San Francisco itself.

240 California St.
415-391-1849
www.tadichgrill.com
Neighborhood: Financial District

TAQUERIA LA CUMBRE

Birthplace of a burrito

Since most San Franciscans are addicted to Mexican cuisine, it's a good thing the city is loaded with taquerias, taco trucks, and restaurants, especially in the Mission District. Taqueria La Cumbre is one such place. It is also one of two places (the other is El Faro) claiming to have invented the Mission-style burrito, the hefty alter ego of your average Mexican roll-up filled with rice, beans, salsa, meat, lettuce, cheese, and guacamole—a gut-busting beauty.

Taqueria La Cumbre was the dream of Raul and Michaela Duran, who emigrated from Mexico to San Francisco in 1967 and opened a meat market. They converted it into a full-time taqueria a few years later. Their son Edward now runs the place and says his dad's motivation for creating the monster burrito was to give local workers a meal they could easily take with them that incorporated the four good groups: grain, dairy, produce, and protein. When the taqueria first opened, flour tortillas were not commercially available, so Raul bought a corn tortilla maker and put it in the basement, and he hired and trained a kid from Mission High School to make flour tortillas on it each morning. That kid was Malo guitarist Jorge Santana, brother of Carlos Santana. He would not be the last famous person to devour a burrito at Taqueria La Cumbre.

Over the past fifty years, TV and movie stars, politicians, and food tour groups have trekked in to chow down. While the

> "We are only as good as our last burrito, so we keep working at making the best."
> ~Edward Duran

Top left: Edward Duran leads tours of his restaurant several times a week. Photo courtesy of Edward Duran

Top right: Grab a Mission-style burrito at its birthplace. Photo courtesy of Kimberley Lovato

Above left: Satisfying San Francisco cravings for decades. Photo courtesy of Kimberley Lovato

Above right: Stuffed with protein, produce, dairy, and grains. Photo courtesy of Kimberley Lovato

attention is nice, and now there are a zillion places to get a burrito in San Francisco, Edward says Taqueria La Cumbre has the same philosophy: be a family-run restaurant sourcing fresh ingredients from longtime suppliers to make authentic Mexican cuisine for everyone. The customers are neighborhood locals who come back week after week, as well as grandkids of people Edward's parents knew. There are even a few out-of-towners, he says, who come back regularly and stock up on burritos before they head to the airport. Tough to explain to TSA, maybe, but well worth the hassle.

515 Valencia St.
415-863-8205
www.taquerialacumbre.com
Neighborhood: Mission

TAWLA

Soulful endeavors

Azhar Hashem grew up in Amman, Jordan, as the daughter of two Palestinian academics. Her mother was an accomplished home cook as well as a headstrong mathematician, and she pushed her three daughters to pursue pragmatic careers. After immigrating with her family to Wellesley, Massachusetts, Azhar attended MIT and earned a computer science degree and then an MBA from Berkeley. What followed was a stratospheric marketing career at Google accompanied by two Emmy Awards, a Clio, and an Effie.

Despite the accolades, Azhar said she was lured away by more "soulful endeavors" inspired by memories of her mother's cooking. Tawla opened in 2016 with former Delfina chef Joseph Magidow charged with developing the menu. "Much of the recipes and inspiration actually came directly from the food I ate growing up. My mother worked closely to help Chef Joe develop some of the recipes that we use every day, to ensure they were right and a true representation of the regions that our menu represents," says Azhar. The flavors, shared histories, and geography of Greece, Turkey, the Levant (the region including Syria, Lebanon, Palestine, Israel, and Jordan), and Iran are shared in items such as the fattoush salad spiced with arugula, sumac, and dates. It's a perfect dish to eat when breaking a fast, says Azhar. Musakhan, an allspice-aged roasted chicken layered with caramelized onions, sumac, saffron, and pine

In Arabic, *tawla* means "backgammon," a game popular throughout the Eastern Mediterranean, and "backgammon," boards are built into tables on Tawla's patio.

Top left: Azhar Hashem. Photo courtesy of Tawla

Top center: Chef Joseph Magidow prepares lamb chops. Photo courtesy of Tawla

Top right: Three Lebanese dips. Photo courtesy of Tawla

Above left: Herbed meatballs with tahini and pine nuts. Photo courtesy of Tawla

Above right: The dining room is as beautiful as the food. Photo courtesy of Tawla

nuts and served with taboon-style flatbread, is the national dish of Palestine. Then there are the snacks that Azhar loved to eat at home—fresh bread dipped in olive oil and za'atar, a Middle Eastern spice mix. What you won't find are hummus, falafel, tabbouleh, or kebab. Instead, curious diners journey on Azhar's soulful quest to share dishes typically missing from Eastern Mediterranean restaurants, and served just the way she remembers.

206 Valencia St.
415-814-2704
www.tawlasf.com
Neighborhood: Mission

TOMMY'S JOYNT

The original hofbrau

You can't miss Tommy's Joynt. This is both an order and an observation. The standout building on the corner of two of San Francisco's main drags, Geary and Van Ness, is covered in colorful murals and has a large neon sign, and the wind whips the flags on the rooftop. It also stands out as the city's original hofbrau. The German word *hofbräu* is linked to breweries and beer gardens where food is served. In California, however, hofbraus are cafeteria-style restaurants typically serving carved meats, a hallmark of Tommy's Joynt.

The namesake is Tommy Harris, a popular local crooner and radio personality, who opened "the Joynt" in 1947. Though it was kept in his family for decades, Tommy's was sold in 2016 to a local restaurateur who promised to keep the San Francisco cult classic the way locals have loved it for the last seventy years. New manager Eddie Martin describes that as "an old San Francisco, blue-collar place for the average guy." It's a place where fancy cocktails don't fly, and where dads bring their sons, just like Grandpa did.

The decor is "stuffed attic meets local pub," and the walls, if you can see them, are covered with sports memorabilia, beer posters, animal heads, old San Francisco photos, and tchotchkes galore. But Tommy's raison d'être is the buffalo stew and the smiling meat carvers who man the cash-only line where up to seven hundred people a day fill up on the slow-cooked pastrami, brisket, corned

Thanksgiving is the busiest day of the year at Tommy's.

Top left: Carlos has been working the bar for more than thirty years. Photo courtesy of Kimberley Lovato

Top right: Carved meats served with a smile. Photo courtesy of Kimberley Lovato

Above left: The building is a landmark on Van Ness. Photo courtesy of Kimberley Lovato

Above right: Tommy's Joynt is San Francisco's original hofbrau. Photo courtesy of Kimberley Lovato

beef, and Tommy's famous turkey, sliced to perfection. The bar offers more than one hundred kinds of beer, which will likely be poured by Carlos Gallegos, a veteran of Tommy's who says he was welcomed in like family when he arrived from Nicaragua in 1982 and given a job. He worked as a busboy, then on the line, and finally moved behind the bar, where he says he perfected his English and loves to talk with regulars and newcomers. Like everything else at Tommy's Joynt, the smiles are generously served.

1101 Geary Blvd.
415-775-4216
www.tommysjoynt.com
Neighborhood: Van Ness

TOMMY'S MEXICAN RESTAURANT

Not your college tequila experience

Raise your hand if, at the mention of the word "tequila," a hazy memory burns its way up your esophagus. Don't worry, you're not alone. It happened to Julio Bermejo many times before he had "the epiphany," which arrived via a glass of Herradura 100 percent agave tequila when he was around sixteen years old. Now older and wiser, Julio manages Tommy's Mexican Restaurant, founded in 1965 by his parents, Tommy and Elmy, who came to California with authentic Mexican and Yucatecan recipes and a dream to open a restaurant.

Tommy's is now a city institution that Julio credits to the incomparable work ethic, good food, and customer-first ethos taught to him by his parents. On most days you'll find Julio greeting regulars by name and serving specialties such as tamales wrapped in banana leaves and pollo pibil. But Tommy's is better known as the home to the Premier Tequila Bar on Earth. That's right, on Earth, Julio insists. Before Tommy's earned this superlative status, the bar had cheap liquor and very little tequila on the menu. Julio says he convinced his father to switch the house pour tequila from a blend to Herradura, which would cost the restaurant significantly more. Julio says he was sure that if he served the best-tasting tequila, people would come

> "If you don't appreciate good tequila after spending an evening with me, then you just don't get it."
> ~Julio Bermejo

Top left: Julio Bermejo now runs the restaurant opened by his parents. Photo courtesy of Kimberley Lovato

Top right: A family-run place since 1965. Photo courtesy of Kimberley Lovato

Above left: Tommy's as a huge tequila collection and club. Photo courtesy of Kimberley Lovato

Above right: Tommy's has stood out on Geary Boulevard since 1965. Photo courtesy of Kimberley Lovato

and learn to appreciate it. That they did. Tommy's not only boasts a worldwide reputation, but it also serves several hundred labels of Mexico's finest. Julio often flies to Jalisco, Mexico, to meet the family-run distillers he sources from, and he founded a tasting club at Tommy's that's now eight thousand members strong.

Try enough tequila and you could earn the title of tequila ninja master or demigod. Julio says he has anointed a number of them. But his ultimate goal is to make sure people eat good food in a family place and never again have a bad tequila experience.

5929 Geary Blvd.
415-387-4747
www.tommysmexican.com
Neighborhood: Richmond

TONGA ROOM & HURRICANE BAR

Get your tiki kicks

You know what they say about fashion: if you wait long enough, everything old in your closet will come back in style. The same can be said of tiki drinks, only in San Francisco, the rum-based concoctions have always been à la mode. Located inside the swanky Fairmont Hotel on Nob Hill, Tonga Room & Hurricane Bar manages to blend Disneyland's Pirates of the Caribbean and a memorable theme party, and has been doing so for seventy years. The menu's selection of Polynesian-flavored items includes ahi tuna poke tostadas, pok-pok wings, and a Tonga pupu platter piled high with an assortment of appetizers.

For cocktails, gone are the cloying drinks of yore, and in their place are handcrafted drinks; a stellar rum collection; and cocktail all-stars such as the Fog Cutter, the original from the bartender Tony Ramos at Hollywood's Don the Beachcomber, and Jungle Bird, created at the Kuala Lumpur Hilton in 1978. But really, people don't come here for the food and drinks. They come here for the food and drinks in *this* setting. Where else can you nosh on pineapple fried rice under a thatched roof while an hourly rain shower, thunder and lightning included, sprinkles a glowing blue lagoon? The "lagoon" is actually the Fairmont's former seventy-five-foot indoor swimming pool, called the Fairmont Terrace Plunge when it was added in 1920.

> The Island Groove Band plays on a barge
> on the lagoon, five nights a week.

Top left: Baby back ribs, yeah baby! Photo courtesy of Tonga Room & Hurricane Bar

Top right: Live entertainment plays on the lagoon. Photo courtesy of Tonga Room & Hurricane Bar

Above left: Entry to Tonga Room & Hurricane Bar is inside the Fairmont Hotel on Nob Hill. Photo courtesy of Tonga Room & Hurricane Bar

Above right: Tiki and Polynesian-themed food are the name of the game. Photo courtesy of Tonga Room & Hurricane Bar

In 1945, the hotel hired film studio Metro Goldwyn Mayer's leading set director, Mel Melvin, to transform the Plunge into a bar. Inspired by the era's tiki trend, he created this San Francisco-meets-the-South Seas fixture that still lures both locals and the famous, including Anthony Bourdain, who filmed an episode of his show *The Layover* here in 2012 and declared his mad love for the place. What more proof do you need that your floral shirt and this temple to tiki are always in style?

Fairmont Hotel, 950 Mason St.
415-772-5278
www.tongaroom.com
Neighborhood: Nob Hill

TONY'S PIZZA NAPOLETANA

Prize-winning pies

It's quite something to be labeled a pizza-making champion, but it's another thing entirely to be the first American (and non-Neapolitan) to earn the title in the birthplace of pizza—Naples, Italy. That's exactly what Tony Gemignani did in 2007, snagging the award in front of thousands of spectators, impressed judges, and some not-so-happy Italian pizzaiolos.

Luckily, you don't have to go that far to taste the prize-winning pie. Just head to North Beach and follow the scent of warm dough. There's a forever line for a table, but it's worth the wait. Inside, you'll find a slew of shiny trophies from other notable victories and a smiling Tony, who hand shapes rounds of dough and, if you're lucky, sends them airborne like floury Frisbees. (He was a champion pizza acrobat, too.) The margherita is the most popular pizza, but the pizza maestro only makes seventy-three per day, a number chosen for Tony's birth year, 1973, and because June 13 (6/13 or 6+1, 3) is St. Anthony's feast day.

The restaurant's seven ovens are used for cooking varied styles of pizza that require different ingredients, techniques, and cooking temperatures. The styles include St. Louis, New York, Sicilian, and even a Detroit-style pizza known for its brick mozzarella cheese and square, crisp crust. Tony prefers the margherita—it reminds him of his honeymoon, he says. Now he tosses dough facing the church

Though Tony has nothing to prove, he still competes regularly.

Top left: No reservations but worth the wait at this North Beach pizzeria. Photo courtesy of Kimberley Lovato

Top right: On top of making a mean pie, Tony Gemignani is also an eight-time world champion pizza acrobat. Photo courtesy of Sara Remington

Above left: Pizza isn't the only thing Tony shows off at his North Beach restaurant. Photo courtesy of Kimberley Lovato

Above right: The prize-winning pizza margherita. Photo courtesy of Sara Remington

in which he was married, in the Italian neighborhood where he walked in parades as a kid, in America's top food city, where he says he'd always wanted his own pizza joint. He's come full circle, one as big as his wagon-wheel-sized pies.

1570 Stockton St.
415-835-9888
www.tonyspizzanapoletana.com
Neighborhood: North Beach

The beat goes on

It is absolutely fair to drop the I-bomb on Tosca Cafe: icon, institution, indelible—they'll all do. Legendary stories swirl about this historic haunt that first opened in 1919, and the people who have bellied up to the bar or slid into the red vinyl booths include the likes of Francis Ford Coppola, Bono, Sean Penn, and Hunter S. Thompson, among other elites.

Tosca lived through the Summer of Love and the Beat Generation. An oversized cappuccino machine never made coffee. The jukebox played only opera tunes. And food stopped coming out of the kitchen in 1953. If there is any place in San Francisco where one wishes the walls could talk, Tosca is it.

When longtime owner Jeannette Etheredge thought she would have to close Tosca, award-winning restaurateur Ken Friedman and equally acclaimed chef April Bloomfield of The Spotted Pig in New York came to the rescue. After sizable renovations, and the knighting of Josh Even as head chef, Tosca reopened in 2013 with a menu of Italian comfort food favorites, such as pasta and red sauce, braised meats, homemade focaccia bread, and roasted chicken for two. The meatballs aren't on the menu, but Josh says to order them anyway. Everyone else does, and they are a best seller. Tosca is the reason Josh returned to San Francisco. He had lived here in his early twenties and says he spent most of his free time at City Lights Bookstore and

> "There was and is no place more uniquely
> San Francisco than Tosca."
> ~Ken Friedman

Top left: Chef Josh Even. Photo courtesy of Sonya Yu

Top right: The old-school flair of the dining room still enchants diners. Photo courtesy of Sonya Yu

Above left: Tosca's bar could tell a story or two. Photo courtesy of Sonya Yu

Above right: Tosca Cafe sign. Photo courtesy of Sonya Yu

Vesuvio Cafe, across the street from Tosca, enamored with the Beat poets. From time to time he'd grab a drink at Tosca.

To be back in San Francisco and at Tosca is both serendipitous and fortunate, says Josh. He only hopes the essence of Tosca never changes. It appears Tosca's plucky soul is safe. The murals might glow brighter, now rid of their smoky grime. The red vinyl booths have been upgraded to leather. And the juke plays rock 'n' roll alongside the opera. But that distinctive anything-goes air is still thick, and it dares a new era of San Franciscans to live up to the legend.

242 Columbus Ave.
415-986-9651
www.toscacafesf.com
Neighborhood: North Beach

Oysters for a cause

One of San Francisco's greatest gluttonous gratifications is a sunny afternoon on the waterside spent sipping white wine and downing fresh oysters. With postcard views of the Bay Bridge and the West Coast's most expansive selection of oysters, Waterbar is the city's premier oyster-slurping perch.

Adding to the allure is that five cents of every oyster sold is given to a variety of Bay Area charities. Managing partner Pete Sittnick says the restaurant started the "Oyster Give Back" campaign in 2014 as a way for the Waterbar team to contribute to the local Bay Area community and, specifically, to coastal causes that complement Waterbar's commitment to offering the freshest and most sustainable seafood available.

To date San Franciscans have gone mollusk mad and eaten enough oysters to donate more than $75,000 to the Marine Mammal Center and the Watershed Project, as well as organizations that work with children, support cancer research, and work to combat homelessness.

399 The Embarcadero
415-284-9922
www.waterbarsf.com
Neighborhood: Embarcadero

"The campaign is our small way of saying,
'We are all in this world together.'"
~Pete Sittnick

Top left: Chef Parke Ulrich of Waterbar serves some of the best seafood in the city. Photo courtesy of Waterbar

Top center: Five cents from every oyster sold at Waterbar is donated to a local charity. Photo courtesy of Waterbar

Top right: Waterbar sits on the Embarcadero near the Bay Bridge. Photo courtesy of Waterbar

Above: The views from Waterbar are postcard worthy. Photo courtesy of Waterbar

YASUKOCHI'S SWEET STOP

Coffee Crunch Cake redux

San Francisco's Japantown sits like an origami flower in the middle of a bustling city, and hidden even deeper away is this gem. Step into the Super Mira market and take a hard right. Tucked away in the corner behind the cases of soda and Lotto ticket machines is Yasukochi's Sweet Stop. The glass case holds a classic collection of pastries and cookies, but what people come for is the Coffee Crunch Cake, an only-in-San Francisco layered sponge cake with whipped-cream frosting covered in crunchy slivers of coffee-flavored candy. The specialty originated at Blum's, a long-gone soda fountain and lunch counter that was big during the '50s and '60s.

The chain closed in the '70s, but not before a former Blum's candy maker taught Tom Yasukochi how to make the coffee lunch candy. He has been making a near-exact replica of Blum's "Koffee Krunch Cake" for more than fifty years now inside his Japantown hideaway.

1790 Sutter St.
415-931-8165
Neighborhood: Japantown

Yasukochi's sells whole cakes or slices,
which often sell out by midday.

Top: Tucked away inside a market, Yasukochi's is a real hidden gem. Photo courtesy of Kimberley Lovato

Above left: Coffee Crunch Cake made daily. Photo courtesy of Kimberley Lovato

Above right: Buy a slice of Coffee Crunch Cake and eat it on the go. Photo courtesy of Kimberley Lovato

YUZUKI JAPANESE EATERY

America's first koji-based restaurant

Yuko Hayashi believes that food (any food) should be shared and enjoyed using all five senses. She also believes it should be healthy, which is why she introduced washoku and a koji-based menu, the only one of its kind in the United States when she opened Yuzuki Japanese Eatery in 2011.

Washoku is traditional Japanese cuisine and comes from the words *wa*, meaning "Japanese" and also "harmony," and *shoku*, meaning "food." It is not just carefully created and exquisitely presented; washoku is also a registered UNESCO Intangible Cultural Heritage of Humanity. The dishes at Yuzuki are almost too beautiful to eat, but go ahead. At once simple and sophisticated, salty and sweet, they are full of clean and complex flavors enhanced by an ingredient that dates back centuries in Japan: koji, a mold similar to yeast that is used to ferment rice or soya beans. Koji allows cooks to use less salt, fat, and sugar while making food tastier with a mild flavor enhanced by amino acids. It also makes food easier to digest.

According to Yuko, in modern-day Japan the technique of koji

"We want people to experience how this food made from scratch is gentle to the body and senses, light and soft."
~Yuko Hayashi

Left: The artistic presentation makes it almost too good to eat. Photo courtesy of Eric Wolfinger

Center: Yuko Hayashi. Photo courtesy of Eric Wolfinger

Right: The airy dining room by day. Photo courtesy of Yuzuki Japanese Eatery

is getting lost because of changing eating habits and ready-made products. Shortly before opening Yuzuki, Yuko discovered a woman named Myoho Asari, a.k.a. "the Kojiya Woman," who is credited with repopularizing koji, in particular salt koji, as an essential ingredient in Japanese kitchens. She was also the muse for Yuko's menu. Many of the regulars who dine in Yuzuki's pristine dining room have lived in Japan or visit several times per year and are happy, says Yuko, to have found the authentic flavors and ancient culture of washoku blossoming in the heart of San Francisco.

598 Guerrero St.
415-556-9898
www.yuzukisf.com
Neighborhood: Mission

California cuisine scene

It is hard to believe this famous epicenter of California cuisine started as a Mexican/Southwestern restaurant when it opened in 1979 at the bottom of a 1913 building. Then-owner Billy West is said to have set up a Weber grill to prepare food, and he called his new café Zuni after the indigenous Pueblo peoples of Arizona and New Mexico. But it wasn't until 1987, when he hired Judy Rodgers as chef and partner, that Zuni went from popular neighborhood hangout to a culinary talisman.

Judy refocused Zuni's menu to an evolving rustic French and Italian flavor, with a mantra of simple, local, and seasonal. She also requested that a brick oven and mesquite grill be put in the restaurant. It is where Zuni's now-famous roast chicken was born. Judy published *The Zuni Café Cookbook*, which won the James Beard Award in 2003, while Zuni Café won the award for Outstanding Restaurant in the country. In 2004, Judy won the James Beard Foundation Award for Outstanding Chef.

Gilbert Pilgram joined Judy as Zuni's second chef-owner in 2006. Judy's death in 2013 devastated San Francisco, her colleagues, and her friends. Teddy Kryger, a server at Zuni, remembers working with Judy and says he feels privileged to have known her. Though he went to cooking school and at one time intended to be a chef, he says he learned more working at Zuni and with Judy than he ever did in school—specifically, how food, simply executed, is enough and that

Many San Francisco restaurants close early, but Zuni serves until 11 p.m. during the week and midnight on weekends.

Top: Zuni is as popular today as ever. Photo courtesy of Bea D'Amico

Above left: The wood-fired oven was added by Judy Rodgers. Photo courtesy of Bea D'Amico

Above right: Teddy Kryger has worked at Zuni for more than sixteen years. Photo courtesy of Teddy Kryger

it is important to support local farms. As a people person, Teddy says once he got a taste for working the front of the house, he was hooked, and sixteen years later he is still pinching himself that he gets to meet regular and international visitors each week and call Zuni his "home." With Gilbert still the chef-owner and Rebecca Boice the executive chef, Zuni continues to execute Judy's vision, energy, and style while bringing the element of surprise to a daily menu, making this city treasure a place that somehow manages to stay perpetually relevant.

1658 Market St.
415-552-2522
www.zunicafe.com
Neighborhood: Hayes Valley

FROM A-Z

1300 on Fillmore
1300 Fillmore St.

AL's Place
1499 Valencia St.

Alfred's Steakhouse
659 Merchant St.

Alioto's
8 Fisherman's Wharf

Anchor Brewing Company
1705 Mariposa St.

AsiaSF
201 Ninth St.

August 1 Five
524 Van Ness Ave.

b. Patisserie
2821 California St.

Beach Chalet Restaurant & Brewery
1000 Great Hwy.

Belcampo
1998 Polk St.

Bi-Rite Market
3639 Eighteenth St.

Blue Plate
3218 Mission St.

Bob's Donuts
1621 Polk St.

BrainWash Cafe & Laundromat
1122 Folsom St.

Brazen Head, The
3166 Buchanan St.

Breakfast at Tiffany's
2499 San Bruno Ave.

Brenda's French Soul Food
652 Polk St.

Buena Vista, The
2765 Hyde St.

Burma Superstar
309 Clement St.

Cafe Zoetrope
916 Kearny St.

Cala
149 Fell St.

Candy Store, The
1507 Vallejo St.

Cheese School of San Francisco, The
2124 Folsom St.

China Live
644 Broadway

Cinderella Russian Bakery & Café
436 Balboa St.

City Counter
115 Sansome St.

Cioppino's
400 Jefferson St.

Cliff House
1090 Point Lobos Ave.

Cookie Love
1488 Pine St.

Dandelion Chocolate
740 Valencia St.

Deli Board
1058 Folsom St.

Doc Ricketts
124 Columbus Ave.

Douglas Room, The
345 Taylor St.

Epicurean Trader, The
401 Courtland Ave.

Ferry Building
1 Ferry Plaza

Fior d'Italia
2237 Mason St.

Forbes Island
Pier 39

Foreign Cinema
2534 Mission St.

Frena Bakery
132 Sixth St.

Golden Gate Fortune Cookie Factory
56 Ross Alley

Ghirardelli Square
900 N. Point St.

Greens
Fort Mason Center, 2 Marina Blvd.

Grove, The
2016 Fillmore St.

Hang Ah Tea Room
1 Pagoda Place

Humphry Slocombe
2790 A Harrison St.

In Situ
151 Third St.

John's Grill
63 Ellis St.

Josey Baker Bread
736 Divisadero St.

La Folie
2316 Polk St.

Lazy Bear
3416 Nineteenth St.

Liguria Bakery
1700 Stockton St.

Lucca Ravioli
1100 Valencia St.

Mee Mee Bakery
1328 Stockton St.

Memphis Minnie's
576 Haight St.

Mensho Tokyo
672 Geary St.

MINA Test Kitchen, The
2120 Greenwich St.

Mission Pie
2901 Mission St.

Mister Jiu's
28 Waverly Place

Mitchell's Ice Cream
688 San Jose Ave.

Nopalito
306 Broderick St.

Off the Grid
Fort Mason Center, 2 Marina Blvd.

Old Clam House, The
299 Bayshore Blvd.

Original Joe's
601 Union St.

Pier 23 Café
Pier 23

Red's Java House
Pier 30

Saint Frank Coffee
2340 Polk St.

Sam's Grill & Seafood Restaurant
374 Bush St.

San Francisco Herb Co.
250 Fourteenth St.

San Francisco Pickle Company
www.sfpickleco.com

Schubert's Bakery
521 Clement St.

SoMa StrEAT Food Park
428 Eleventh St.

Song Tea & Ceramics
2120 Sutter St.

Sour Flour
2937 Twenty-Fourth St.

Sotto Mare
552 Green St.

Starbelly
3583 Sixteenth St.

Swan Oyster Depot
1517 Polk St.

Taco Shop @ Underdogs, The
1824 Irving St.

Tadich Grill
240 California St.

Taqueria La Cumbre
515 Valencia St.

Tartine Bakery
600 Guerrero St.

Tawla
206 Valencia St.

Thanh Long
4101 Judah St.

Tommy's Joynt
1101 Geary Blvd.

Tommy's Mexican Restaurant
5929 Geary Blvd.

Tonga Room & Hurricane Bar
Fairmont Hotel, 950 Mason St.

Tony's Pizza Napoletana
1570 Stockton St.

Tosca Cafe
242 Columbus Ave.

Waterbar
399 The Embarcadero

Woodhouse Fish Co.
1914 Fillmore St.

Yasukochi's Sweet Stop
1790 Sutter St.

Yuzuki Japanese Eatery
598 Guerrero St.

Zuni Café
1658 Market St.

ESTABLISHMENTS BY NEIGHBORHOOD

POLK GULCH

Bob's Donuts, 28
Swan Oyster Depot, 176
La Folie, 108

PORTOLA

Breakfast at Tiffany's, 34

POTRERO HILL

Anchor Brewing Company, 10

RICHMOND

Burma Superstar, 40
Tommy's Mexican Restaurant, 188

RUSSIAN HILL

Belcampo, 22
Candy Store, The, 46
Saint Frank Coffee, 158

SEA CLIFF

Cliff House, 58

SOMA (SOUTH OF MARKET)

AsiaSF, 12
BrainWash Cafe & Laundromat, 30
Deli Board, 68
Frena Bakery, 88
In Situ, 102
SoMa StrEAT Food Park, 168

TENDERLOIN

UNION SQUARE

VAN NESS/CIVIC CENTER